Across the Land and the Water

Across the Land and the Water

Selected Poems, 1964–2001

W. G. SEBALD

Translated from the German
by Iain Galbraith

HAMISH HAMILTON
an imprint of
PENGUIN BOOKS

HAMISH HAMILTON

Published by the Penguin Group
Penguin Books Ltd, 80 Strand, London WC2R 0RL, England
Penguin Group (USA) Inc., 375 Hudson Street, New York, New York 10014, USA
Penguin Group (Canada), 90 Eglinton Avenue East, Suite 700, Toronto, Ontario, Canada M4P 2Y3
(a division of Pearson Penguin Canada Inc.)
Penguin Ireland, 25 St Stephen's Green, Dublin 2, Ireland (a division of Penguin Books Ltd)
Penguin Group (Australia), 250 Camberwell Road, Camberwell, Victoria 3124, Australia
(a division of Pearson Australia Group Pty Ltd)
Penguin Books India Pvt Ltd, 11 Community Centre, Panchsheel Park, New Delhi – 110 017, India
Penguin Group (NZ), 67 Apollo Drive, Rosedale, Auckland 0632, New Zealand
(a division of Pearson New Zealand Ltd)
Penguin Books (South Africa) (Pty) Ltd, 24 Sturdee Avenue, Rosebank,
Johannesburg 2196, South Africa

Penguin Books Ltd, Registered Offices: 80 Strand, London WC2R 0RL, England

www.penguin.com

First published in German by Carl Hanser Verlag 2008
Published in English with additional material by Hamish Hamilton 2011
2

Set in Perpetua 14/17 pt
Typeset by Palimpsest Book Production Limited, Falkirk, Stirlingshire
Printed in Great Britain by Clays Ltd, St Ives plc

A CIP catalogue record for this book is available from the British Library

ISBN: 978-0-241-14473-2

www.greenpenguin.co.uk

Contents

School Latin

Appendix

Translator's Introduction

'My medium is prose,' W. G. Sebald once declared in an interview, a statement easily misconstrued if a subtle distinction the German author added is overlooked: '. . . not the novel'. Far from disavowing his attraction to poetic forms, Sebald's sworn allegiance to what he called 'prose' deliberately placed his work at arm's length from the generic exactions (plot, character development, dialogue) levied by the more conventional modes of writing fiction. Indeed it is perhaps only in reading Sebald's poetry, whose breathing and tone, especially in the later poems, frequently recall the timbre of the narrative voices in *Vertigo*, *The Emigrants* or *The Rings of Saturn*, that we may begin to sense the poetic consistency of his literary prose itself – in fact that of his writing as a whole. Equally, reversing the focus, readers of W. G. Sebald's prose fiction who come to his shorter poetry for the first time may be surprised to find that many of the concerns of his acclaimed later prose works are prefigured even in his earliest, most lyrical poems: borders, journeys, archives, landscapes, reading, time, memory, myth, legend, and the 'median state' (to use Edward Said's term) of the exile, who is neither fully integrated into the new system nor fully free of the old. Following the development of the poetry from its lyrical beginnings to the later narrative forms, we can trace the trajectory of the author's gradual reach for the epic scope of his work in the 1990s, a quest which, as I wish to argue, initially culminated in the tripartite, book-length, narrative poem *Nach der Natur* (*After Nature*, 1988). On the way, we shall discover poems to value for their singular artistic achievements: some puzzling, some dazzlingly hermetic, others deceptively slight or simple, several witty or ironic, each in its different way an encounter with life's unresolved questions and mysteries, each gazing into the abyss of twentieth-century European history.

W. G. Sebald began publishing poetry as a student in the 1960s, and he continued to write poems throughout his life, publishing many in German and Austrian literary magazines. Among the work he had prepared for publication shortly before his untimely death in 2001 were the poetry volumes *For Years Now* and *Unerzählt* (*Unrecounted*), while a host of shorter poems he had intended to publish in the 1970s and 1980s did not come to light until after their posthumous removal to the German Literature Archive in Marbach. Before completing his first major literary work, *Nach der Natur*, in the mid-1980s, Sebald had prepared and paginated, apparently for publication, two collections of shorter poems – 'Schullatein' ('School Latin') and 'Über das

Land und das Wasser' ('Across the Land and the Water'),
consisting altogether of some ninety poems – neither of
which would find its way into print. Leaving aside work
that has already appeared in English in the volumes *After
Nature*, *Unrecounted* and *For Years Now*, the present
selection of W. G. Sebald's poetry offers a representative
viewing of work from the two unpublished volumes,
while at the same time collecting almost all of the
shorter poems published in books and journals during
his lifetime, including, in an appendix, two poems
written by the author in English and published in 2000 in
the Norwich-based literary journal *Pretext*. Readers may
be curious to compare Sebald's own English poems with
those which have found their way into English through
acts of translation – setting the author's writing in a
foreign tongue against foreign translations from his
mother tongue.

The present volume presents Sebald's poetic
production from the poems and publications of his
student years ('Poemtrees'), across the two unpublished
volumes already mentioned, through to the narrative
forms of the 1990s and turn of the millennium (gathered
in the section 'The Year before Last'). Of the eighty-eight
poems published here in translation for the first time,
thirty-three draw on unpublished* manuscripts deposited
for the Estate of W. G. Sebald at the German Literature

---

*The original German poems will appear in the journal *Akzente* in
December 2011.

Archive, while fifty-five are translations of poems in the German volume *Über das Land und das Wasser* (*Across the Land and the Water*), edited by Sven Meyer in 2008. The question naturally arises as to why W. G. Sebald did not publish 'School Latin' or 'Across the Land and the Water' after their completion, probably in 1975 and 1984 respectively. There may be no single answer to this question, but one explanation points to what could be called an 'epic' or 'narrative' turn in Sebald's writing during the mid-1980s. In order to understand how this came about, it is necessary briefly to describe the sequence and composition of some of the manuscripts deposited in the writer's archive in Marbach.

Sebald's papers, as we shall see, reveal the movement of his poetic work since the mid-1960s as a kind of 'rolling' project or cascade, culminating in the publication of *Nach der Natur* (*After Nature*) in 1988. Significantly, however, the three sections of the latter volume were completed rather earlier, with the middle section probably completed by 1984. It is likely that this and the following year were decisive, marking both the moment of Sebald's transit to longer narrative forms, and, simultaneously, the provisional curtailment of his plan to publish a volume of shorter poems. The three sections of *Nach der Natur* first appeared in the Austrian journal *Manuskripte*: 'And if I Remained by the Outermost Sea' (October, 1984), 'As the Snow on the Alps' (June, 1986) and 'Dark Night Sallies Forth' (March, 1987). Michael

Hamburger's English translation *After Nature*, whose three sections I have cited here, was published in 2002.

What the papers in the Marbach archive show us is that W. G. Sebald's typescript volume 'School Latin' inherited poems from an even earlier, albeit more fragmentary file: 'Poemtrees', more a loose bundle of poems than a collection. Twelve poems from this earliest grouping, included in the present volume as the first twelve translations of the section 'Poemtrees', represent Sebald's earliest publications of all, appearing in a Freiburg students' magazine (1964–5). The collection 'School Latin', in turn, supplied seventeen poems – many of them in revised versions – to the subsequent collection 'Across the Land and the Water'. Similarly, the final section of the latter volume, consisting of the full text of 'And if I Remained by the Outermost Sea', went on to form the second of the three sections of *After Nature*. Furthermore, the third and final section of *After Nature* ('Dark Night Sallies Forth') incorporates, as a perusal of the archive reveals, at least eighteen shorter poems, half of them in their entirety, and all of them cut from the typescript of 'Across the Land and the Water'. These texts, in as far as they were whole poems pasted verbatim into the final section of *After Nature*, have not been included in the present volume.

To conclude: Sebald's decision, in 1984, to publish the final section of 'Across the Land and the Water' in *Manuskripte*, and – possibly in the same year – to allow

'Dark Night Sallies Forth' to 'cannibalize' the shorter
poems of 'Across the Land and the Water', heralded the
beginning of an entirely new poetic project, paving the
way for the completed typescript of the tripartite
narrative poem *Nach der Natur* to be sent to various
publishers from November 1985 (as we learn from a list
of submissions to publishers filed in Sebald's archive). At
the same time, however, the concomitant attenuation of
the 'Über das Land und das Wasser' typescript effectively
ended any plans the author may have harboured to
publish a collection of poems based on the material
assembled since 'Poemtrees'. Some readers may agree
with W. G. Sebald that prose was the medium to which
his hand was best suited. Poems written after the mid-
1980s, however, not only make it clear that poetry
remained an important medium to Sebald until the end
of his life, as volumes such as *For Years Now* and *Unerzählt*
(*Unrecounted*) attest, but also suggest that, had events
unfolded differently, he might have returned to the
project of assembling a volume – one that would surely
have included many of the later poems in the present
collection.

W. G. Sebald's poems present the translator with a
number of quandaries, at least one of which does not
derive from disparities between the English and German
languages, or directly from the poet's wide-ranging
allusiveness. The problem I am referring to arises

because the translation – in bodying forth a poem that claims to address exactly the same subject as the poem does in German, and even to represent the author's language – has no choice but to turn itself into a vehicle of the very difficulties that may have prompted Sebald's poem in the first place. This is most evident in relation to two of the German poet's perennial and interrelated concerns: reading and memory. Many of Sebald's poems, for example, address elisions, or repression and suppression of memory, texts and other forms of discourse. However sincerely motivated, however 'close' to the source, the translation of a poem 'perpetrates' just such elision. For in order to offer the best possible guidance to a text in the course of its hazardous transformation in the new hermeneutic environment the translator must change not merely a few items, but *every single word* of the poem. Even names – Kunigunde, Badenweiler, Landsberg, Hindenburg – have a different sound or suggest different connotations, and are likely to be read from a specifically different perspective in the 'target language'.

Entry to a new cultural context transfigures the poem and evidently regenerates its testimony. It may be argued, however, that this difficulty merely leads to a frequently visited aporia – that logical cul-de-sac whose sole outcome is to posit the impossibility of translation – and that by redefining the boundaries of the problem we can liberate the translator from the cavil of misrepresentation. For does not the poem itself – which the translation, by some sleight of hand, actually pretends to be, and whose movement it purports to re-enact – construct perspectives from which it will be read, opening certain routes to the understanding of its world and consequently eliding others? And does not the poem encourage as many readings as it has readers? The translation, inventing the original word by word (for without a translation there is no original), follows the 'hard act' of the poem, rebuilding its place in a new terrain. In so doing, it harbours the hope that as many new readings of the poem will be added as those which, inevitably, have been lost. For in the end, the survival and continuing promise of the poem depends on just such access to new and engaging environments of intellectual sophistication and skilful acts of reading.

'Reading' in Sebald's poetry, however, is a process that not only responds to text. His poems read paintings, towns, buildings, landscapes, dreams and historical figures. The consequence is an encyclopaedic wealth of literary allusion and cultural reference, much of which may not be named in the text itself. Sebald's sentences can not only contain pitfalls but thread an uncomfortably narrow ledge along the abyss of what, in one poem, he calls 'the history / of torture à travers les âges' ('Bleston'). The difficulties this creates for the translator are self-evident. Words are by nature as precise as they are ambiguous, and the translator must in each case explore their field of reference, resonance and determination in the source text and language before deciding on one word rather than another in the new text. In the case of Sebald's poems such explorations can prove long and complex, leading the explorer to a plethora of attendant historical and cultural 'dark matter', in relation to which the poem itself may appear deceptively straightforward and even slight. Sometimes, this 'dark matter' – however aware the translator needs to be of its existence – does not, in the end, affect the words of a translation in any pivotal way. Allow me to offer an example that will take us into the heart of the difficulty of translating – and that is, essentially, reading – Sebald's poetry.

Many of the poems in the present volume – which opens with a train journey – re-enact travel 'across' various kinds of land and water (even if the latter is only the fluid of dreams). Indeed, several, as the writer's archive reveals, were actually written 'on the road', penned on hotel stationery, menus, the backs of theatre programmes, in cities that Sebald visited. Train journeys constitute the most frequently recorded mode of travel. The following poem may refer to one such journey. 'Irgendwo', translated in English as 'Somewhere', was probably written in the later 1990s and originally belonged to the sequence of 'micropoems' that provided the material for Sebald's posthumous collection *Unerzählt* (*Unrecounted*), published in 2003:

Somewhere

behind Türkenfeld
a spruce nursery
a pond in the
moor on which
the March ice
is slowly melting

With its evocation of a wintery landscape and suggestion
of a thaw on its way this apparently simple poem seems
nothing short of idyllic. The invitation to research
possible frames of reference is emitted solely by the
place-name, Türkenfeld: a small town, indeed hardly
more than a village, in the Fürstenfeldbruck area of
Upper Bavaria, a place-name on the so-called Allgäu line,
a route Sebald will have taken often enough between
Sonthofen, where his family moved from Wertach in
1952, and Munich.

However, it is well if a translator is aware that
landscapes in Sebald's work are rarely as innocent as they
seem. The phrase 'behind Türkenfeld' is itself already an
indication of 'how hard it is' – in the words of what
could almost be read as a programmatic poem opening
the present collection – 'to understand the landscape /
as you pass in a train / from here to there / and mutely

it / watches you vanish.' In this metaphorical sense the poem puts the traveller's gaze itself at the centre of its encounter with a cryptic landscape, exploring the difficulty of inciting a historical topography to return that gaze by divulging its secrets. Many of Sebald's poems enact the battle of the intellect and senses with the hermetic or repellent face of history's surface layers. The impression is one of travelling across a land in which the catastrophic events of the twentieth century have left a pattern of shallow graves under an almost pathologically hygienic and tidy upper stratum of civilization. What, then, is 'behind' Türkenfeld?

The only thing this 'mute' landscape divulges to the traveller-reader is its name, a sign linking the idyll of the poem to the 'dark matter' of its cultural-historical ambience. The poem itself shows us only the unsettled gaze. To the close reader of landscapes, however, the name itself is enough to admit the 'cold draught' (the title of another poem more visibly 'freighted' than this one) of a relatively recent, yet already almost forgotten history into the space of the poem. Research tells us that one of the ninety-four sub-camps of the concentration camp at Dachau was constructed in Türkenfeld, though it was never used. The surrounding landscape is the site of the eleven external camps of the Kaufering network of satellite camps. These were set up to facilitate arms manufacture in caverns and caves in an effort to evade Allied bombing, the geological composition of the

Landsberg area proving favourable to construction of massive underground installations. Türkenfeld was formerly a station on the Allgäubahn, and the railway linking Dachau with Kaufering and Landsberg, known as the 'Blutbahn' (the blood track), passed through Türkenfeld. As many as 28,838 Jewish prisoners were transported along this line from Auschwitz and Dachau to Kaufering to work as slaves on the construction of the underground aircraft plants Diana II and Walnuß II. Some 14,500 died in the plant or were deported, when they had become too weak to work, back through Türkenfeld to the gas chambers. Our first unknowing reading of the poem, and with it the poem's own translation of an unruffled, apparently unremarkable landscape 'mutely' watching us 'vanish', points to the perilous consequences of our loss of cultural memory. 'To perceive the aura of an object we look at,' wrote Walter Benjamin, referring more to works of art than to landscapes, 'means to invest it with the ability to look at us in return.' Our struggle to 'understand' the mute historical holdings of Sebald's poetic landscapes in passing – a form of engagement his poems frequently invite the reader to explore – brings us face to face with our failure to make the crucial investment that Benjamin describes.

In translating this volume I have enjoyed the advice, experience and expertise of several people I should like to thank here. First and foremost of these is Sven Meyer, the editor of the German volume *Über das Land und das Wasser*, published by Hanser Verlag in Munich, whose groundbreaking work paved my own path to the Marbach archives. I have discussed aspects of W. G. Sebald's poetry and writing life with a number of the author's friends and colleagues, including Philippa Comber; Thomas Honickel; the late Michael Hamburger; Anne Beresford; the author's friend during his Freiburg student days, Albrecht Rasche; the young poet's colleague at the University of Manchester in 1966 and 1967, Reinbert Tabbert; also his later colleague at the University of East Anglia, Jo Catling. To all of them I am indebted for their helpful, and often extensive, responses to my queries. I am grateful to Volkmar Vogt of the Archiv Soziale Bewegung for supplying me with copies of Sebald's early publications in the journal *Freiburger Studenten-Zeitung*, to the Estate of W. G. Sebald and the staff of the German Literature Archive in Marbach for giving their support to this project, and also to the Institute for Advanced Studies in the Humanities in Edinburgh, where some of the initial work for this volume was undertaken. Last but not least I owe a special debt to Karen Leeder, who kindly provided critical comments, invaluable to me, on early drafts of the translations that follow.

Iain Galbraith

Note on the Text

In the translations that follow, punctuation and orthography (e. g. in proper nouns) are generally coherent with the author's typescripts, as held in the W. G. Sebald Archive at the Deutsches Literaturarchiv, Marbach, or, in the case of material already published in German, with the texts of poems in journals and books, as sourced in the notes that conclude the volume. Accordingly, occasional irregularities or punctuational inconsistencies in the source texts have been retained in the present edition. Words and phrases which appear in English in the German poems are identified in the endnotes.

Poemtrees

For how hard it is
to understand the landscape
as you pass in a train
from here to there
and mutely it
watches you vanish.

A colony of allotments
uphill into the fall.
Dead leaves swept
into heaps.
Soon – on Saturday –
a man will
set them alight.

Smoke will stir
no more, no more
the trees, now
evening closes
on the colours of the village.
An end is come
to the workings of shadow.
The response of the landscape
expects no answer.

The intention is sealed
of preserved signs.
Come through rain
the address has smudged.
Suppose the 'return'
at the end of the letter!
Sometimes, held to the light,
it reads: 'of the soul'.

Nymphenburg

Hedges have grown
over palace and court.
A forgotten era
of fountains and chandeliers
behind façades,
serenades and strings,
the colours of the *mauves*.
The guides mutter
through sandalwood halls
of the Wishing Table
in the libraries
of princes past.

Epitaph

On duty
on a stretch in the Alpine foothills
the railway clerk considers the essence
of the tear-off calendar.

With bowed back
Rosary Hour
waits outside
for admittance to the house

The clerk knows:
he must take home
this interval
without delay

Schattwald in Tyrol

The signs are gathered
settled at dusk's edge
carved in wood
bled and blackened
printed on the mountain

Hawthorn in the hedgerow
along a length of path
black against winter's papyrus
the Rosetta Stone

In the house of shadows
where the legend rises
the deciphering begins
Things are different
from the way they seem
Confusion
among fellow travellers
was ever the norm

Hang up your hat
in the halfway house

Remembered Triptych of a Journey from Brussels

White over the vineyard by Sankt Georgen
white falls the snow across the courtyard and on
the label of an orange-crate from Palestine.
White over black is the blossom of the trees
near Meran in Ezra's hanging garden.
Autumn in mind April waits
in the memory for painted walnut
like the life of Francis of Assisi.

At the end of September on the
battlefield at Waterloo fallow grass grows
over the blood of the lost Marie-Louises
of Empereur Bonaparte
you can get there by bus
at the Petite-Espinette stop
change for Huizingen
a stately home, sheltered by ivy, transformed
into the Belgian Royal Ornithological
Research and Observation Unit
of the University of Brussels.

On the steps I met Monsieur Serge Creuve,
painter, and his wife Dunja —
he does portraits in red chalk on rough paper

of rich people's children
from Genesius-Rhode. – Lures them into the house
with the unique WC, well-known
to neighbours. – One does like to visit an artist.
'Shall we buy the *ferme* in Genappe?'

In the evening at Rhode-St Genèse
a timid vegetable man carries his wares
up garden paths past savage dogs
to the gate, for instance, of the Marquise of O.'s villa.
A woman's mouth is always killed
by roses.

As a lodger on the third floor
 – the red sisal only goes up to the second –
of Mme Müller's Cafeteria
five minutes' walk from the Bois de la Cambre
I'm the successor to Robert Stehmer
student from Marshall Missouri.
Gold-rimmed jug-and-bowl on the dresser
a hunting scene over the Vertiko cabinet
door to an east-facing balcony. – At night
noises on of the road to Charleroi.

Chestnuts fell from their husks
in the rain.
I saw them in the morning
glossy on the sand of the patio.

I saw them in the morning –
taking tea and Cook Swiss
to be eaten with a knife and fork.
I saw them in the morning
waiting behind the curtain
for a trip to town
in quest of Brueghel
at the Musée Royal.

Départ quai huit minuit seize
le train pour Milan via St Gotthard
I recognized Luxembourg by the leaves on its trees
then came industrie chimique near Thionville,
light above the heavenly vaults
Bahnhof von Metz, Strasbourg Cathedral
bien éclairée. – Between thresholds
lines from Gregorius, the guote sündaere,
from Au near Freiburg, rechtsrheinisch,
not visible from Colmar – Haut Rhin.
Early morning in Basel, printed on
hand-made Rhine-washed lumpy paper
under the supervision of Erasmus of Rotterdam
by Froben & Company, fifteen hundred and six.
Men on military service bound for Balsthal in the Jura
shaved and cropped, several smoking,
outside all changed.

Route of all images
light grey river-sand
ruddy hair minding
swollen shadows
lances and willows
White leaf, you
Green leaf, me
Rafael, Yoknapatawpha,
Light in August
between leaves
anxious mellowing
before birth
as a shadow
over the sunny road

Go to the Aegean
to Santorini
Land of basalt
phosphorescence on the rudder
Hold the water
in your hand:
it glows – at night –
aubergines in front of the house
shadowy in the dark
against the whitewashed wall
bright green in daytime purple
raffia-threaded
in the sun.

Life is Beautiful

Days when
At the crack of dawn
The early bird
Squats in my kitchen.
It shows me the worm
Which sooner than later
Will lead me up the garden path.
I've already bought
My pig in a poke
It's all Tom or dick
Kids or caboodle
In the home and castle.
My day is truly
Wrecked.

Matins for G.

There he stood
In the early morn
And wanted in.
It's warm
In front of the fire.
Lug a-cock
The man waited
For some response
To his knock.
Came a bawl from within:
Jesus Mary
A pain in the neck
In the early morn.
Where no kitchen
There no cook.
We don't need no
King.
The man has heard
As much before.
He has heard enough.
Right then: all or nothing.

Winter Poem

The valley resounds
With the sound of the stars
With the vast stillness
Over snow and forest.

The cows are in their byre.
God is in his heaven.
Child Jesus in Flanders.
Believe and be saved.
The Three Wise Men
Are walking the earth.

Lines for an Album

Quick as a wink, a star
Falls from heaven
Like nothing
That grows on trees.
Now make a wish
But don't tell a soul
Or it won't come true
Ready or not
Here I come!

Bleston
A Mancunian Cantical

1. Fête nocturne

I know there exists
A shuttered world mute
And without image but for example
The starlings have forgotten their old life
No longer flying back to the south
Staying in Bleston all winter
In the snowless lightless month
Of December swarming during the day
From soot-covered trees, thousands of them
In the sky over All Saints Park
Screaming at night in the heart
In the brain of the city huddled together
Sleepless on the sills of Lewis's Big Warehouse
Between Victorian patterns
And roses life was a matter
Of death and cast its shadows
Now that death is all of life
I wish to inquire
Into the whereabouts of the dead
Animals none of which I have ever seen

ii. Consensus Omnium

In eternity perhaps
All we experience
Becomes bitter Bleston
Founded by Gn. Agricola
Between seventy and eighty AD
Appears in the ensuing
Era to have been
A bleak and forsaken place
Bleston knows an hour
Between summer and winter
Which never passes and that
Is my plan for a time
Without beginning or end
Bleston Mamucium Place of
Breast-like hills
The weather changes
It is late in our year
Dis Manibus Mamucium
Hoc faciendum curavi

III. The Sound of Music

An unfamiliar lament
And the astonishment that
Sadness exists – one's own
Never the other of those who suffer
Of those whose right it really is
Life is uncomplaining in view of the history
Of torture à travers les âges Bleston
Uncomplaining is this mythology without gods
The mere shadow of a feast-day phantom
Of a defunct feast-day Bleston
From time to time the howls
Of animals in the zoological
Department reach my ears
While I hold in my hands
The burnt husks of burnt chestnuts
The silence of revelation
Sharon's Full Gospel – the sick are
Miraculously healed before our eyes
The ships lie offshore
Waiting in the fog

iv. Lingua Mortua

He couldn't help it Kebad Kenya
If the years of all humanity lay
Strewn about him in their thousands debris
Erratic and glacial white in the moonlight
Reclining in silence on the river of time
Hipasos of Metapontum by the Gulf of Tarentum
Made bronze discs of varying thickness ring out
Five hundred years before Christ
Et pulsae referunt ad sidera valles –
It was Pythagoras however of whom it was said
He possessed the secret of listening to the stars
The valleys of Bleston do not echo
And with them is no more returning
Word without answer fil d'Ariane until your blood
Hunts you down with opgekilte schottns
Alma quies optata veni nam sic sine vita
Vivere quam suave est sic sine morte mori
Only in the wasteland does Rapunzel find bliss
With the blind man Bleston my ashes
In the wind of your dreams

v. Perdu dans ces filaments

But the certitude nonetheless
That a human heart
Can be crushed – Eli Eli
The choice between Talmud and Torah
Is hard and there is no relying
On Bleston's libraries
Where for years now I have sought
With my hands and eyes the misplaced
Books which so they say Mr Dewey's
International classification system
With all its numbers still cannot record
A World Bibliography of Bibliographies
On ne doit plus dormir says Pascal
A revision of all books at the core
Of the volcano has been long overdue
In this cave within a cave
No glance back to the future survives
Reading star-signs in winter one must
Cut from pollard willows on snowless fields
Flutes of death for Bleston

Didsbury

Sunday was fed
Up to the teeth
With church bells
Summer hats
Gardening

Birds were squabbling
Over Lord knows what
Among the withered
Chestnut blossom

The presbyter went
To his May devotions
And it took
A long time
To get dark

Before it did
The birds made
A din
In the trees

Giulietta's Birthday

The French windows
Are open still
As if in the theatre
People wait
On the colours of the carpet
In the cadence of dusk

Irony it is said
Is a form of humility

Glass in hand
They come and go
Stop still and expect
The metamorphosis of hawthorn
In the garden outside

Time measures
Nothing but itself

In the courtyard of a monastery in Holland
My name escaped me
Early in life according to Scott

Swift had acquired the habit
Of celebrating his birthday
In dejection

One leaves behind one's portrait
Without intent

Time Signal at Twelve

for Lejzer Ajchenrand

His eyes
Home in
On the real

There is
Skulduggery
Afoot

A raven alights
At God's ear
Tidings he brings
Of the battlefield

Father has gone to war
The monk from Melk
Sleeps in his quiet grave
The snow
Falls on his house

If no one asks him
He knows
But if someone asks him

He knows not
When the Weisers
Will meet

Something not a soul
Has ever seen

Children's Song

for little Solveig

Fieldwards goes the day
Mildew grows in the garden
Measles cover the man
Like a thousand butterflies

Fieldwards goes the day
Long long ago
Studded with stars was the sky
A thousand butterflies

Come from the fields is a day
A coachman stands at the bone-house
Holding in his hands
The thousand butterflies

School Latin

Votive Tablet

Weary of always
the same trees and
a country far from crossed
the legionnaire rests
in fancy's meagre holding

Revolving around him by turns
his life and a bloom of tobacco
smoked by the wayside

The hammered out sections
show him whenever he moves
which of his organs
alas are sick

Cheerful after all
humbly sat on his shield
he bids us good day
the one-eyed
king of the blind

Legacy

Our memories are quite similar
but pickled alive
in a poison which

accompanies objects too
as a part of this emptiness

The heartening message
that Pythagoras once
would listen to the stars
barely comes down to us now

Then let us hope
our children are learning
to dance in the dark

Sarassani

With borrowed voices
the ventriloquist renders
others' pipe-dreams

A gentleman disguised
as a moth pulls
tropical birds from a hat

The gaudiest parrot
weighs a memorized
word destiny
in his hand

As accustomed dupes
the local fowls
sit in the cheap seats
thrilling to the da capo

Day's Residue

Dialectically thrashed out campaigns
and drafts from days
pending wasted battles

Like every evening
the set task is left
undone in the sandpit

Heeding a dubious silence
I sleep at night
with my ear to the ground

Its distant sounds
spell out
the lessons of a lighter world

Border Crosser

My beard grows overnight
every time
like a dead man's

I have even begun
to speak in foreign tongues
roaming like a nomad in my own
town weighing the witch's
thaler in my hand

It would seem to be time
to apply to the outworks
and register what
we have forgotten

Once there
given the superior outlook
my poor sedentariness
will pass

Lay of Ill Luck

In honour of my canny schoolmate
and god of wonders
I had promised a
Chinese fable

In crow's-feet characters
the black bird
translated itself
nimbly to my page

The little vixen however
escaped and tumbled
in the grass and all
but laughed herself to death

So all I have left
is this monosyllabic
creature on my shoulder

Memorandum of the Divan

The mightiest however
seem those kings
who have never lived

Even today
they tempt us
on tours
to Soliman's garden
on a horse
with clipped wings

To comfort the bereaved
it is advisable that reports of such trips
be prepared in advance

For it will often have proved
far too lovely to return
in any calculable future

Il ritorno d'Ulisse

Returning from a lengthy trip
he was astonished to find
he had strayed to a country
not his place of origin

For all his encounters in scattered spots
with the black paper hearts of men
shot by the arquebuse
his bow-and-arrow story
did not happen

Then there was Penelope's
Castilian grandmother
blocking his entry at the garden gate
wordless and busy with embroidery

Sure, the grandchildren
are smiling in the background
apparently better disposed
towards foreigners

Their furtive hopes
still almost too small
for the naked eye

(But the idea is good
and the noise far away
even the building)

For a Northern Reader

Until the light has
failed as if bereft
the white mist
barely infiltrating
the trees

and as if they were painted
on a green landscape the animals
descending to their black shelters
come to a standstill
at the edge of our gaze

resolute
half his journey done
our ailing neighbour too
pauses
reckoning the distance left

Florean Exercise

The band was playing
and singing a little Turkish
marching song, with ensigns
shouldered they filed out
onto the plain at their ease
to where their ships lay
concealed beneath the cliffs

Their camp has long
been abandoned the soldiers
long ago returning to an older
post in a different time

But in Northamptonshire
their legacy has remained
green acanthus and orchards
houses inhabited still
by the Roman gaze

Guarding what once
was brought here
safely from afar
the Dardanian gods

Scythian Journey

Faced with the deep shadows
of the mountains of growing darkness
we had to break our journey

Making ourselves at home
high in the canopy of the forest
with the birds and fishes

Discussing the dragging winter
and maybe blowing a tune
on the Berecyntian horn

Savouring our dawdling
the poor Penates
smile among themselves

Saumur, selon Valéry

The beginners have concluded
an exercise in the accomplishment
of elaborate figures
as part of their training
in advanced impromptus

Abandoned now
the sand-track curves
into the lengthening shadows

Then, slipping through subito
from some other place an apparition
crosses our field of vision
at an astonishingly measured tread

Démonstration, Messieurs,
the zenith of my art,
riding, at a walk, and
that without flaw
or flourish

Says almost imperceptibly
bending down towards us
prior to vanishing
at the other side
Chiron the old centaur

L'instruction du roy

The real disaster
so they say are the consolations
the *garde bourgeoise*
in the republic of our dreams

Repetition once mere play
a five-finger exercise suddenly
a repertorial must
for intractable pupils

To cheer people up
they shift the scenes now and then
in our moral institutions

The mountain backcloth sinks
into the waves and time sheds
its skin every year

Out of sorts in the stalls
the Troubadour beholds
the panoptic spectacle while
poised at the entrance
Malatesta forks out for his ticket

Festifal

Setting:
On the Sandwich Islands
the Dictaean Grotto

Personae:
Basil the Rainmaker
and the coiled polar dragon

Plot:
Somnia, terrores magicos,
miracula, sagas, nocturnos
lemures portentaque Thessala

Intermezzo:
Acts of negligence in accordance
with relative beauty
strength or wit
  ex. gratis: The plump Etruscan,
     the ivory flute
     and Latin song
     aut:
     Proteus sub aqua submersus
     putting ugly cattle to pasture
     aut etiam:

The Sphinx
fleeing toward Libya

Final Tableau:
Victorious Basil
earns the sobriquet Fifty

Analysis:
Salomo Schellenkönig the skilled
basket weaver counts his coppers

Balance:
A small
fortune

Pneumatological[1] Prose

Recently seen
in the vicinity of Flore
Northants, the rhinoceros
appeared this morning
in my garden

With a sly look albeit somewhat
nonplussed it stood in the herbs
wreaking as it shifted its weight
from one foot to the other
considerable havoc

    The animal is a victor
    the elephant's mortal foe
    for when he comes upon it
    the beast will charge headfirst
    between its front legs

    They also say
    the rhinoceros
    is quick, joyful and
    lusty too

Odd to say it did not retire
to the bushes after its wont
but with its head arrogantly
cocked on one side ascended
skywards in a gaily embroidered
Californian moored balloon[2]

A monotheistical
creature it would seem
while the elephant
as Pliny tells us
is clever and just
and worships the sun
and the moon

1. Pneumatology: *Geisterlehre* (Germ.), or Doctrine of
Inflatability.
2. Large and very handsome flying and sailing device constructed
by Messrs H. and C. Artmann, Royal Engineers.

Comic Opera

The programme enlists the turqueries
of a newly lapsed century
a potpourri with bells and cymbals
orchestrated obscenities

Masked players swell
the plot in a green theatre
their true faces overwritten

Rather than greater virtue
the happy ending proposes
more trivial vices

The hedges rustle with applause
and the bygone ladies
of the court return
below the lawns

Back to reading
cubist
novels

Timetable

Grown sheepish
by morning I study
the grounds of my coffee

At midday I cut
a slice for myself
from the hollow pumpkin of summer

And not until dark do I risk again
the Cretan trick
of leaping between the horns

Unexplored

Great-grandfather
in his gay jacket
casting a horoscope

A perfect
heptagram omitting
the malefic houses

Those white areas
photoset and printed
in my historical atlas

Elizabethan

As you know
the owl was only
a baker's daughter

And Sheikh Subir
a professor expelled
from Persia

Baroque Psalter

After numerous
proselytizing expeditions
to Paris
Geneva Smyrna and
Constantinople
he was burned at the stake
in Moscow

Across the Land and the Water

Cold Draught

Surrounded by German
mothers and conscript
sons homeward on the
Bundesbahn: the leaning

tower by Landsberg
the murder at Hotel Hahn
the Buchloe cheese factory
the lunatics of Kaufbeuren
the abbey school windows
the abyss of childhood

And in the dark
lifting her skirts
Saint Elizabeth
stepping daintily
over glowing ploughshares

Near Crailsheim

Precisely undulated fields
little globular trees
sculpted and dark green
pedantically aligned
rows of maize

Thereabove to the west
God's pleasure
pink candyfloss
from the recent funfair

Mumbling the enigma of their
crosswords pensioners sit
on the express, limbs benumbed
in the quicksilver of their angst

Already the shadows are smoking
in the valley of Jehoshaphat
Here comes the railwayman
his lamp bouncing on his bib

Poor Summer in Franconia

The poster in the village shop
recalls the yellowed terror
of the Colorado beetle

In the backroom behind her
the shopkeeper's children sit glued
to the nation's wooden eye

Windfalls lie leaden in the garden
and blue in the crayfish-stream
flow the suds from the washing machine

The Moor on the hill
peeps from an American tank
among the dying spruces

In the afternoon
my crazy grandfather
torches the fields

My last aspirin
dissolves gently
in a glass

As the pain subsides
I hear once more
the call of the distant posthorn

Solnhofen

White fields
in winter sometimes
strewn with ash

The high shoulders of the hill
stunted conifers
juniper shrubs
rock tombs
one-eyed sheep

Overtaken by ruin
a Wilhelmine artisan mill
reflects the breadlessness
of the passing trains

Deposited between layers
lie the winged
vertebrates
of prehistory

Leaving Bavaria

Glacial in the early morning
the train station at Bamberg
a Reichspost stamp
overprinted for hyperinflation

Hindenburg's grey-green millions
history's null ouvert
penny panic
in the poor souls of commuters

Beyond the tracks
moored in the half light
the brickwork brewery
a German airship

At the gondola window
Saint Dionysius
a lonely passenger
with his head under his arm

Something in My Ear

Falling asleep
on the sofa
I hear from a distance
geese on the radio
whetting their beaks
to pass the verdict

The mildew grows
in the garden paralysis
spreads
a long succession
of minute shocks
I feel the blood
at the roots
of my teeth

As I awake
sudden cardiac
death waves
from the other side
of the abyss

Panacea

A snip of the scissors
a thimble
a needle's eye

A place of pilgrimage
a memory stone
a mountain moved

A club moss
and a cube of ice
tinted with a jot
of Berlin blue

Mithraic

Nine thousand nine hundred
and ninety-nine years
Zarvan murmured
to get a son

And now his descendants
are flogging off
the houses of heaven
and the five coasts of the earth

With his sea-goat ready
for departure the mythologist
beholds once again
the shattered world egg

Memo

Build fire and read
the future in smoke

Carry out ash and
scatter over head

Be sure
not to look back

Attempt
the art of metamorphosis

Paint face
with cinnabar

As a sign
of grief

Barometer Reading

Nothing can be inferred
from the forecasts

Tree frogs
are ignoring their ladders

Changeable weather tests the patience
of the rheumatic soul

The slightest gust makes it flutter
first this way then that

Meanwhile Propertius
waits faithfully in his folding boat

One oar in the water
the other skimming the sand at the edge

K.'s Emigration

His personal effects
are ready to leave

Entered
well in advance
the calligraphic endorsement
an analphabetic cipher
valid for a single journey

Pictures sent
en route greetings
from Bohemian Switzerland
and a group photo
in front of the High Tatras

Didn't you
have your
photograph taken
in Franzensbad too

Through Holland in the Dark

The cucumbers
lurk in their greenhouses

The customs official
borrows my evening paper

A wet hand
casts no shadow

Kaiser Willem
is still smoking his cigars

No sign
of the reclaimed land

Abandoned

like Kafka's essay
on Goethe's abominable
nature

Mölkerbastei

Beethoven's room
is tidy now

The pictures straightened
the curtains washed
and week for week the floors
polished anew

But the chair
for the grand
has been taken away

He still comes in at night sometimes
and composes something
standing up

The proviso is
it be audible only
with an ear-trumpet

A Galley Lies off Helsingborg

Such desolation
in Harwich harbour
when I am here
it always seems to me
as if we were
in the throes of a silent war

The hollow barges
all that bulky
worn-out iron
the oil-green water
and the ever stiller
county of Essex
round about

The poor travellers
with their woe-begone
faces oppressed
hapless folk
standing here waiting
on the Red Sea shore

Nobody tells them
where the ferries are heading for
tonight

Holkham Gap

A green zone
for field glasses
and camouflaged
ornithologists

Beyond it the bay
its sweep broader
than the furthest
horizon

The Home Guard
waited here
for the sea lion
to appear

When the monster didn't
show the marram
was permitted to reoccupy
the fortified strip

But Uncle Toby
doesn't entirely
trust the peace

Stuffing his pillow
with sand he wishes
the deluge would begin

Norfolk

Sailing backwards
as a passenger with
banished time

A Louisianian
landscape populated
by invisible windmillers

Where the Egyptian
in his painted boat
sails between fields

Crossing the Water

In early November 1980
walking across
the Bridge of Peace I almost
went out of my mind

Natural History

In Man it is
the Quadruped
in Woman the Amphibian
who has the upper Hand

Ballad

Is Carl Löwe's
heart
really
immured
in a column
in the Church of St James
in Stettin?

Obscure Passage

Aristotle did not
apprehend at all
the word he found
in Archytas

Poetry for an Album

Feelings my friend
wrote Schumann
are stars which guide us
only when the sky is clear
but reason is a
magnetic needle
driving our ship on
till it shatters on the rocks

It was when my palsied
finger stopped me playing
the piano that calamity
came upon me

If you knew every cranny
of my heart
you would yet be ignorant
of the pain my happy
memories bring

Carnaval time for the children
with friends dressed up
as Ormuzd and Ariman
fleecy clouds of gold
melting in the pure ether

For years now I've had
this same whistling
sound in my ears
and it troubles me greatly

Walking by the Rhine
I know I shall steer
for the North I have yearned for
though it be colder there
even than the ice on
geometry's intersecting lines

Eerie Effects of the Hell Valley Wind on My Nerves

In the cathedral square
of a town he left
many years ago
the emigrant sits
reading the secret history
of Judge Dr Daniel Paul Schreber

Events of war within
a life cracks
across the Order of the World
spreading from Cassiopeia
a diffuse pain reaching into
the upturned leaves on the trees

The black holes
of ghosts flying about
in the sky above
conceal as I know
li più reconditi principii
della naturale filosofia

Come lacklustre times, you
in the midst of beauty
of obscenity my nights

will help you remember
a pale block of ice
slowly melting

The judge speaks
I am the stony guest
come from afar
and I think I am dead

Open these pages, he says,
and step smartly
into hell

Unidentified Flying Objects

Late last night
I was standing in the garden
when a space ship
sparkling with lights
passed incredibly
slowly
over our roof

What can you do
but watch the ocean giant
pull away beyond the trees
and head for another galaxy

In sixty-nine
on Pwllheli beach
in Wales I saw a small
glimmering object
sink gently humming
in the air as it floated
down from the top
of a mountain that was printed
entirely in Japanese colours
finally vanishing
over the vast sea

What on earth it was
or what that ship was
yesterday in the sky
I cannot imagine
perhaps it was the soul
of the Welsh prince
slain by his brother
by the lake of Idwal
over which no bird
has flown since

The Sky at Night

A belated excursion to
the stone collection
of our feelings

Little left here
worth showing
alas

Is there
from an anthropological perspective
a need for love

Or merely for
yearnings easy
to disappoint

Which stars
go down
as white dwarfs

What relation
does a heavy heart bear
to the art of comedy

Does the hunter
Orion have answers
to such questions

Or are they
too closely guarded
by the Dog Star

A Peaceable Kingdom

Like an early geographer
I paint a lion or two
or some other
wild animal
in my white
memory fields

Porcupine, chameleon
flounder and grouse
jackal and unicorn
xanthos and mouse .

Outside with the real
birds screaming in the dark
they stand guard
figuring with their
tiny heads what is
still to come
before the sun
goes out

Crocodile, monkey
buffalo, hare
dromedary, leopard
mud turtle, bear

Is it enough
to be overcome
by feeling
at a few words
in our children's
school primer

Are these the emblems
of our love

Trigonometry of the Spheres

In his year of mourning
Grandfather moved
the piano to the attic
and never brought it
down again

With his brass telescope
he now explores
the arcs of the heavens instead

His logbook records
a comet with a tail
and the categorical proposition
that the moon is the earth's work of art

From him I also know
of the holy man who sits
where night turns to day
roaring like a lion

And once he said do not forget
the north wind brings
light from the house of Aries
to the apple trees

Day Return

I

Feeding carefully through the junctions
the early train slips
through the station precincts
a tatzelwurm en route for the city

Riveted grey of the iron bridges
and coming through mist
a peaceful canal
with a barque
from which the Hunter Gracchus
has already stepped ashore

Views to the rear
of inferior housing
wooden sheds tin roofs
dog kennels gutted
cars and tiny
home-made crystal palaces
hung with tomato plants
last year's hopes

The power station in the outskirts
lying on its back
a sick elephant
still just breathing
through its trunk

The little gold-toothed priest
facing me buries himself
in the news of the day
the ink of the godless
staining the little pink fingers
of a furry day-blind animal

Who scrawled the warning
Hands off Caroline
across the fire-wall
in Ipswich who knows the names
of our brothers the ducks
under the willow on the island
in Chelmsford Park pond

Who knows the noises
made by the animals
in Romford at night
and who will teach
the King's starling
to whistle a new song

Pulling into the north-easterly
quarters of the metropolis
Gilderson's Funeral Service
Merton's Rubbish Disposal
the A1 Wastepaper Company
Stratford the forest of Arden
and the first colonists
on the platform at Maryland
heavenly Jerusalem
skyline of the City
brick-wall catacombs
Liverpool Street Station

II

The city sinks behind me
as I head home in the evening
reading Samuel Pepys's diary
of the Great Fire of London

People taking to boats
many pigeons killed
panic on the river
looting near Lincoln's Inn
Bishop Baybrooke's corpse exposed
fragments blown to Windsor Park

The tatzelwurm passes through the country
nightly shadows hedges and fields
and in the darkness gently
glowing the elephant now
so utterly different

New Jersey Journey

Spent two hours at the end of December
on the Garden State Highway
In the ancient Ford's trunk
nothing but my heart grown
heavier year by year

A protracted catastrophe:
the constant river of traffic
the endless business of overtaking
vicious eye-contact
with total strangers
in the adjacent lane

Driven by yearning
for its prehistoric brothers
a Jumbo climbs out of Newark
airport over marshes and lagoons
a giant smoking
mountain of rubbish
and the countless lights
of the refineries

Mile after mile of stunted trees
telegraph poles fields of blueberries
a Siberian countryside
colonized then run to seed
with moribund supermarkets
abandoned poultry farms
haunted by millions and millions
of breakfast eggs
harbouring the undeciphered sighs
of an entire nation

Near the retirement town of Lakehurst
a safari park soundless
under its coat of frost
cemeteries as spacious
as the world war killing fields
funeral parlours dubious
antique shops and a bus station
for last trips
to Atlantic City

In the twilight of the settlement itself
ten square miles of faintly
luminous bungalows
lawns dwarf-conifers
Christmas decorations

Santa Rudolph the Reindeer
and in front of one of the houses
my uncle feeding the songbirds

Drinking schnapps
he later tells me
of the conquest of New York
Drinking schnapps I consider
the ramifications of our calamity
and the meaning of the picture
that shows him, my uncle
as a tinsmith's assistant in '23
on the new copper roof
of the Augsburg synagogue
those were the days

Next day we drive out to the coast
Seaside Park Avenue at noon
the boardwalks deserted
boarded-up diners
Alpine-style summerhouses
with circulating draughts
yachts rattling in the cold
the sub-urban migration of dunes

With the brown house-high waves
in the background my uncle
leaning forward into the wind

snapped me again
with his Polaroid

Do we really die
only once

The Year before Last

The Year before Last

For some time
we crossed a low plateau.
Our eyes took in
the distant landscape,
elegant touring cars
flew past
and a motor-cyclist
with a gun
over his shoulder
appeared again and again
in our mirror.

Soon our road curved down
swiftly into a basin and
Marienbad lay suddenly before us,
a petrified magical city.
Black spruces thronged
to the edge of the outer buildings,
Siberian chervil and eight-foot
giant hogweed in the gardens.
Behind the drab, yellow façades:
Old German furniture,
hat boxes, the strains of a pianola,
an inkling of poison and bile.

It was like driving
into an old-time theatre.

We had a fire made up in the hotel
although it was still mid-summer.
Later, wrapped in heavy
Scottish dressing-gowns we gazed
through the open windows
and gloomy rain outside
into a dusky otherworld.
Is not the world here still,
you asked; do banks of green
no longer follow the river
through bush and lea? Does
not the harvest ripen? Do
holy shades
no longer hang
upon the cliffs? Is this
drawing-in
the grey stain of night?

Next day we sat in the café
beneath a painting of water-lilies. Or
perhaps they were even flamingos.
Do you remember the waiter?
His closely cropped white hair,
his turn-of-the-century
frock-coat and taffeta bow?

The way he kept touching
his left temple with his fingers?
Remember the Cuban cigarettes
he brought me? The fine blue
smoke rose straight as a candle.
A good sign, no doubt.
And indeed, outside it had turned
brighter. Reduced aristocrats
swished past in dust-cloaks
bound for the refectory.

The Rabbi of Belz, plastic
beaker in hand, walked to the well.
A bride and groom were posing
for a photograph on the promenade.
Harquebused suffering
hearts lay about
on the shorn lawns.
Returning to the hotel
we saw Dr K, half-obscured
by a red flag, sitting
at his balcony table,
busy with a portion
of smoked pork much
too big for him

The match game
was meant to decide everything.

The gleaming parquet floor
stretched before us. All round us
were mirrors, guests, motionless —
and in the middle you
in your feather boa. Hadn't
we met once before?
In a taxus maze?
On a stage? The perspectival
prospect, pruned hedges,
little round trees and balustrades,
the palace in the background?
You were supposed to say, I
am wholly yours, nothing
but these words;
and you did say them,
while strangely not
coming an inch
closer.

During the journey home
fantasies of a fatal accident.
Unspectacular woodlands
and hills flanking our route
through the countryside.
The motor-cyclist
turns up again in our rear.
Not a soul on the streets
of Eger. I see only

one woman shovelling coal
through a cellar hatch.
A deserted house,
the icy cold here,
the corridors and chambers,
the flight from the alcove,
the blind window-pane,
the flash of a lance,
the barely audible cry of horror.
And at the end of the act
they carry the pierced
corpse across the stage
in a piece of crimson tapestry.

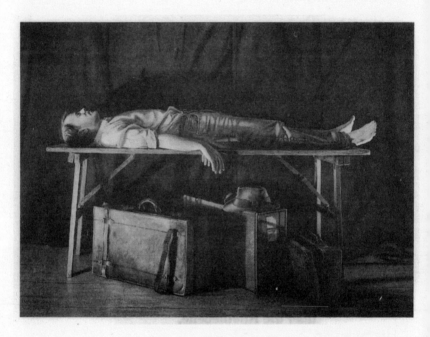

Jan Peter Tripp, *The Land of Smiles*, 1990.

A Waltz Dream

The traveller
has finally arrived
at the border post

A customs official
has untied his laces
removed his shoes

His luggage rests
abandoned on the
planed floorboards

His pigskin suitcase
gapes, his poor
soul has flown

His body, last
of his personal effects
awaits meticulous scrutiny

Dr Tulp will soon be here
in his black hat, prosectorial
instruments in hand

Or is the body already
hollow and weightless,
floating, barely

guided by fingertips,
across to the land
one may only enter barefoot?

Donderdag

23 Februari 1995
between Schiphol
& Frankfurt at ten
thousand feet
in the air
I read a
report in the
paper about
the so-called
carnavalsmoorden

van Venlo all
about the strange
quarter of Genooy
where in the van
Postelstraat
right among
the respectable
condos stands
a row of
whorehouses

where white & coloured
women sit

behind the
windows & where
a few guys from
the koffieshop
branche: Frankie
Hacibey & Suleyman
drive out
one evening to an

execution on the banks
of the Maas. There is
talk of a
bludgeon & a
bread knife of
a jar containing
thirty-five
thousand guilder
& of the married
couple Sjeng &

Freda van Rijn who
as the carnival
surged through
the town centre
were lying at home
twee oude mensen
met doorgesneden
keel op de grund

a dark tale which
so they say has much

to do with hashish
dealing Turkse
gemeenschap &
Duitse clientèle
with greed & ven
geance violence
een zwarte Merce
des een rode BMW
& twee kogels van
dichtbij in het hoofd.

The secrets

of the Universe,
Patriotic Tales and
Memorabilia,
A Germanic
Hall of Fame,
The Neudamm
Forester's Primer,
Register of
Germany's
Protected Species,
Social Hygiene
in Hamburg
and The Mushrooms
of our Region –

all informative
work assembled
by chance
in the display
of a junk shop
near a railway
underpass in
Oldenburg I

think or Osnabrück
or in some
other town

30.IX.95

On 9 June 1904

according to the Julian
calendar, on 22 June
according to our own,
Anton Pavlovich and
Olga Leonardovna reach
the spa at Badenweiler.

The tariff is sixteen marks
for board and lodging
at the Villa Friederike
but the spelt porridge
and creamy cocoa
bring no improvement.

Suffering from emphysema
he spends all day
in a reclining chair
in the garden marvelling
again and again at how
oddly quiet it is indoors.

Later in the month the weather
is unusually hot, not
a breath of wind, the woods

on the hills utterly still,
the distant river valley
in a milky haze.

On the 28th Olga travels
to Freiburg specially
to buy a light flannel
suit. At the Angelus hour
of the following day
he has his first attack, the

second the following night.
The dying man, already
buried deep in his pillows,
mutters that German
women have such
abominable taste in dress.

As dawn breaks
the doctor, placing
ice on his heart,
prescribes morphine
and a glass of champagne.
He was thinking of returning

home with Austrian
Lloyd via Marseille
and Odessa. Instead

they will have him transferred
in a green, refrigerated
freight car marked

FOR OYSTERS
in big letters. Thus has
he fallen among dead
molluscs, like them packed
in a box, dumbly rolling
across the continent.

When the corpse arrives
at Nikolayevsky Station
in Moscow a band
is playing a Janissary
piece in front of
General Keller's

coffin, also newly
arrived from Manchuria,
and the poet's relatives
and friends, a small
circle of mourners,
which from a distance

resembles a black
velvet caterpillar,
move off, as many

recalled, to the strains
of a slow march
in the wrong direction.

Ninety years later

on a Sunday after-
noon in the month
of November I drove
south from Freiburg
across the foothills
of the Black Forest.

All the way down
to the Belfort Gap
low motionless clouds
above a landscape
deep in shadow,
the hatched patterning

of vineyards on the slopes.
Badenweiler looks
depopulated after
some virulent summer
epidemic. Silent
haemorrhaging in every

house, I guess, and
now not a living
soul about, even

the parking lot
near the facilities empty.
Only in the arboretum

under giant
sequoias do I meet
a solitary lady
smelling of patchouli
and carrying a white
Pomeranian in her arms.

As the evening
draws in the sun
sinks in the West
between the clouds
and the skyline of
the Vosges hills

the last of the
fading light flooding
the Rhine plain
which shimmers and quivers
like the salty shore
of a dried out lake.

In Bamberg

I lie sleepless
in a stone-built
house. The last
revellers have
abandoned the streets
and, save for
the Regnitz rushing
over the weir
there is hush.

Whirlpools drag me
under the water
and I roll along
the bed of the river
with the stones
a gasping fish
I return to the
surface, my eyes
wide with fear.

The passage of dreams
is haunted by ghosts
the Little Hunchback
for example standing

by the sluice hut
on the Ludwig Canal. He
wears glasses
with uncannily
thick lenses and

a blue base-
ball cap
with the logo
MARTINIQUE
back to front
on his head.
Empress Kunigunde
has been waiting
for ever

at the foot
of the Katzenberg
and on the bridge over
to the old Town Hall
of which an oleograph
always hung
in our sitting-room
the dog Berganza
crosses my path

for the third time.
A little way

further upstream
up at the Hain
Park Schorsch
and Rosa are taking
a stroll one August
afternoon in '43
she in a light

dust-cloak he
with his traditional jacket
slung over his
shoulder. They
both seem happy
to me, carefree
at least and a good
deal younger than
I am now.

Thus, thinks
Kara Ben Nemsi
son of the German,
floweth time
a ruby red
cipher leaping
from digit to digit
trickling
in silence

from the dark
of night
to the grey
of dawn
just as sand
once ran
through
the hour
glass.

May 1996
May 1997

Marienbad Elegy

I can see him now
striding through the suite
of three south-westerly
facing rooms in his
cinnamon-coloured
coat pondering

diverse matters
for example his long-
harboured plan
for a treatise on clouds
& yet somewhat
troubled too

& testy on account of
his passion for Ulrike
who is the reason
for his third visit
to this up-&-coming
resort. He looks

out at the little
rotund trees
evenly spaced around

the square in front of
the Kebelsberg Palais,
sees a gardener

pushing a barrow
uphill, a pair of blackbirds
on the lawn. He has slept
badly in the narrow
bed & felt like some
beetle or other strange

creature till outside
dawn spread
its wings & he could
rise & continue
his work. True, he'd
give anything now to

rest again but any
minute now they would
call him to table.
Perhaps they'll serve
a pike, then escalope
& to finish a compote

of wild berries.
Bohemians know a thing
or two about cooking:

the sweet dumplings with
his morning coffee were a joy
& his dearest beloved seemed

so gentle again, of such
delicate humour &
fondness for himself he
all but died of
loving hope & felt his
heart throb in his throat.

Thus the days pass.
He gazes into
her eyes & twists
his finely embroidered
napkin wallet
once to the left

once to the right.
When his request for
her daughter's hand
is met with reluctance
by her mother & after
the last cruelly sweet

kiss he departs
in a sombre mood
through the mountains &

still in his coach composes
the famous elegy
of twenty-three stanzas

which in the manner
of his own telling
is said to have leapt from
a tempest of feeling
the ripest creation
of his old age.

As for me however
I have never really
liked this gorgeous
braid of interwoven desires
which the poet upon
arriving home

had transcribed in his
most elegant hand
& personally bound
in a cover of red
morocco tied
around with a ribbon

of silk. I saw its
facsimile in the Marienbad
Museum this morning

along with several other
objects which meant
much more to me

& among which was
a wick trimmer
& a set of sealing
waxes, a little
papier mâché tray
& an ink drawing

on pasteboard by Ulrike
showing in somewhat uncertain
perspective the North-
Bohemian village of
Trebívlice where she lived
as a spinster until her

death. Further
a China-yellow
tulip-poplar leaf
from her herbarium
inscribed in black ink
across its thin veins

then the sad remains
of black lace to which
Czech gives the lovely

name *krajky*, a kind of
choker or cravat &
two wristlets not

unlike muffetees &
so narrow that her wrist
cannot have been
much stronger than
a small child's. Then
there is a steel engraving

showing Fräulein von
Levetzow in her declining
years. By now her
former suitor has
long lain under the soil
& here she stands

in a grey taffeta
dress next to a book
table, with an abominable
bonnet-full of
corkscrew curls &
a ghostly-white face.

Marienbad, 14.VIII.99

At the edge

of its vision
the dog still sees
everything as it was
in the beginning

And always

toward the East
the corn
blindingly white
like a firn-field
at home

How silvery

on that
January morning
the towers
of Frankfurt
soared
into the ice-cold
air

Somewhere

behind Türkenfeld
a spruce nursery
a pond in the
moor on which
the March ice
is slowly melting

In the sleepless

small hours
of Sunday 16th
January last
year in the hideously
rustic Hotel
Columbus in Bremer
haven I was set
upon with whoops
& squawks by the four
Town Musicians. The
terror still in my
limbs I sat on
the dot of eight
alone but for my
morning coffee &
jaundiced by the light
coming in through
the bull's-eye panes
of the guest house.
Past the window
on the wet cobbles
outside filed the
shadows of emigrants
with their bundles & packages

people from Kaunas
& Bromberg from the
Hunsrück & Upper
Palatinate. Over the
loudspeaker came the soft
strains of that same
old accordion the
same old singer's
voice quavering
with emotion forgotten
poesey of our people
the home star &
the sailor's heart. Later
from the train the Powder
Tower from Nibelung
days the coffee
silos block-hoards of
brown gold on the
horizon a satellite
town before it a colony
of allotments once
maybe known as Roseneck
Samoa or Boer's
Land. And over
the North German
plains motionless for
weeks now these
low blue-black

clouds the Weser
flooding its banks
& somewhere around
Osnabrück or Oldenburg
on a patch of grass
in front of a farm
a lone goose
slowly twisting its
neck to follow
the Intercity
careering past.

Room 645

Hotel Schweizer
hof, in Hinüber
Straße Hannover

a table-top
composed like a jig-
saw of various

exotic & home-
grown timbers
finished with a cover

of marbled faux
leather. On the walls
greenish dotted

textured paper &
a picture composition
by Karsten Krebs with

Sogni di Venezia
beneath it in silver
script. The carpet

is spotted with midnight
blue the velvet
curtain is claret the

sofa ultra
marine the bedspread
calyx motif

turquoise with a
dizzying arabesque
in lilac & violet

on the bedside rugs.
Through the grey
net curtain the

view of an ugly
tower block the
TV-tower

the coal-black
Sparkasse-building
its top storey

with the S-logo
& saver's penny.
Nothing happens

all day until
towards evening
stretched across

the entire re
inforced glass
window a ragged

flight of crows
makes wing
to its roost.

My ICE Rail-Planner

Herrenhausen is offering
a cruise to Denmark two
visits to the seawater wave-
bath thrown in someone
will be waiting at the station
& will say how nice

to meet you & how
about a Fitness-Week
in Eckernförde. Outside
the light is thinning the
ribbon of a road glistening
in the drizzle black

patches of forest & off
white farmsteads
pass, in a lime
works over the hills
stone is being ground to
dust. We are wired

I read to the vital nerves
of our national economy
radio, transmission &

defence systems
office communications
railways & building components

ready & waiting for you.
Simply phone or fax
us this coupon. At some
point during the hour
between Fulda & Frankfurt
it had started to get dark

& where a moment before
there had been blue
landscape I saw in their
rows beside me the
reflections of the heads
of my tired fellow

travellers gliding
on through the night. Thus
spake the angel of
the Lord: Fear not
for our house is kept to
the highest standards

& has a pleasant
ambience. Gall-bladder
liver stomach

intestines metabolic
disorders overweight
ageing impairments

rheumatism please
write for our prospectus
& ask your chemist for
the energy-vitamin for
executives especially
those over forty.

One Sunday in Autumn 94

I am in the unmanned
station in Wolfenbüttel
waiting for the railcar
from Göttingen to
Brunswick. Fleecy
clouds fleck the sky
sporadic leaves spin
from the trees an old-
timer in brown breeches
rides a lady's bike
across the tracks. Hearing

the bells ring I recall
the cathedral at Naumburg
the minsters of Ulm &
Freiburg the Church of Our
Dear Lady in Munich
long-forgotten Hogmanays
& other catastrophes.
The Herzog August Video
Rental a one-window-fits-
all semolina-coloured
establishment is closed but

the kiosk between the doner-
shop & the Wellaform
hair-salon is open
to anyone in a hurry
to purchase the *Bild-
Zeitung* or a porn mag.
In the yard in front
by a lattice fence
overgrown with
pink roses stands
a small gathering of

all-weather drinkers
in beards & baseball-
caps like gold diggers
from the Australian outback.
Their bottle of Chantré
does the rounds while
from an election poster
on an advertising column
the Father of the German
Nation gazes anxiously
on his reunified country.

Calm November weather

in Germany persistently
foggy & dull. Bottom temperatures
from zero to three degrees
with low cloud cover

over Brandenburg & Berlin.
A cold sea breeze from
the north sweeps across
the square where once

the Lustgarten lay with
its symmetry of Prussian
precision a fountain
to left & right, white

diagonal gravel paths
an equestrian monument
at the exact centre & lawns
that are out of bounds.

That says my guide
is the cathedral
sixteen Hohenzollerns
lie under the sand

in fact this ground
is steeped in history
they find corpses
every time they dig.

The ravens on yonder
grass patch know what
they are after. The S-Bahn
winds out of the chasm

between the Pergamon
& Bode Museums
a bright streak high
on the bridge another

below in the dark
waters of the Spree.
At the train station
which is wrapped in

plastic sheeting we
say goodbye. She returns
to Brüderstraße while
I set off to Wannsee

there to stay
the night at the literary

villa & for the very
first time ever

witness a living
Greenlandic
poet in the flesh.
Called Jessie

Kleemann she stands
in a blaze of
floodlights in
her red velvet suit

her pale oriental-
looking face in
front of the penumbral
figures of the audience

her lips whispering
into the microphone
forming sounds
that consist it

seems to me of
nothing but double
vowels & double
vees sliding up &

down the scale the
sounds of her feathery
language taavvi
jjuaq she says the

great darkness &
lifting her arm
qaavmaaq the
shimmering light.

Unchanged for years

now these inter-
regional catering
clichés the full
buffet breakfast
the sliced cheese
the boiled ham
the scrambled eggs
the nutty nougat
crème the stew of
the day the hearty
goulash the Nuremberg
Bratwurst the potato
salad the burger

with bread-roll
grandma's beef
olives your favourite
choc-bar the salted
peanut De Beukelaer's
chocolate-filled
cookies the Nordhäuser
Doppelkorn the age-old
Asbach the finesses of
Gau Köngernheimer

Vogelsang &
the Rotkäppchen
dry.

In the Summer of 1836

said the guide
Friedrich Chopin
stayed here at the White
Swan Inn. It had

taken him nine
days from Paris by coach
to reach his beloved
Marie Wodzińska. He

gave frequent recitals
on the piano to a small
circle who gathered in
the evenings. The peaks

of the blue Bohemian
mountains grow
ever darker through
the window. The cold

damp weather weighs
on his chest the doctor
mumbles something about
incipient tuberculosis. At

the beginning of November
their engagement is shattered
her father in Dresden has
put his foot down.

Thirteen years later
a packet of faded
letters is found in the
deceased pianist's

residence. Tied with
ribbon it carries the
inscription: Moja
Bieda – My sorrow.

In Alfermée

late in November
the rain sweeps
down from the Jura
throughout the night

Threading sleep
letter by letter
comes a language
you do not understand

The exhausted eyes
of the writer the fingers
of one hand on the
keys of her machine

Darkness lifts
from the earth in the morning
leaving no difference
between lake & air

Along the shore
is a row of poplars
behind them a lone boat
at a buoy

Beyond the grey
water invisible
through swathes of mist
the village of Sutz

a few lights
going out &
a column of snow-
white smoke.

On the Eve of

All Hallows
nineteen hundred
and ninety-seven at
Schiphol Airport

among globetrotters
from Seoul & Saõ Paulo
Singapore & Seattle.
There they sit

with neon-blue
faces slumped
down on the benches
rummaging now

& then distractedly
in their luggage not
one of them uttering
a spoken word. With

the witching hour
past they lie
stretched out under
blue blankets

asleep while outside
the fog gradually
shifts revealing
once again

through the darkness
the runways & lit
steps the enormous
bodies & tail

fins of the vessels
lying at anchor
at their quays. Not
a single movement

around me now
only the sparrows
who have survived
for years in this

part of the terminal
whirr back &
forth across the hall
& up & down

the arcade settling
in the green palms
& ficus trees
jerking their little

heads this way &
that looking out
between the artificial
leaves with their shiny

black eyes &
chattering raucously among
themselves as if something
were not quite right.

In the Paradise Landscape

of the younger Brueghel
on a surface roughly
thirty by forty

centimetres in size
before which I stood
for a time at the Städel

Museum all manner
of beasts & birds
have come together

in peace an eagle
owl with horned
ears an ostrich

with button eyes &
a strangely flat
beak a billy

goat & a few sheep
two polecats or martens
a wolf a horse

a peacock a turkey
& in the foreground
at the bottom edge

two spectacled
monkeys one of which
is gingerly plucking

strawberries from a little
shrub while on the right
roses climb

an apple or pomegranate
tree & tulips
in full blossom

& spring stars &
lilies & hyacinths
& somewhat in the background

in a choice act
of man-manly
procreation our Lord

& Creator a tiny
& obscure figure
barely visible

to the naked eye
bends over
Adam sleeping

on a grassy bank
& cuts from his side
his bride to be.

Appendix

Two poems written in English by W. G. Sebald

I remember

the day in
the year after
the fall of the
Soviet Empire

I shared a cabin
on the ferry
to the Hoek
of Holland with

a lorry driver
from Wolverhampton.
He & twenty
others were

taking super-
annuated trucks
to Russia but
other than that

he had no idea
where they were
heading. The gaffer
was in control &

anyway it was
an adventure
good money & all
the driver said

smoking a Golden
Holborn in the upper
bunk before
going to sleep.

I can still hear
him softly snoring
through the night,
see him at dawn

climb down the
ladder: big gut
black underpants,
put on his sweat-

shirt, baseball
hat, get into
jeans & trainers,
zip up his

plastic holdall,
rub his stubbled
face with both his
hands ready

for the journey.
I'll have a
wash in Russia
he said. I

wished him the
best of British. He
replied been good
to meet you Max.

October Heat Wave

From the flyover
that leads down
to the Holland
Tunnel I saw
the red disc
of the sun
rising over the
promised city.

By the early
afternoon the
thermometer
reached eighty-
five & a steel
blue haze
hung about the
shimmering towers

whilst at the White
House Conference
on Climate the
President listened
to experts talking

about converting
green algae into
clean fuel & I lay

in my darkened
hotel room near
Gramercy Park
dreaming through
the roar of Manhattan
of a great river
rushing into
a cataract.

In the evening
at a reception
I stood by an open
French window
& pitied the
crippled tree
that grew in a
tub in the yard.

Practically defo-
liated it was
of an uncertain
species, its trunk
& its branches

wound round with
strings of tiny
electric bulbs.

A young woman
came up to me
& said that al-
though on vacation
she had spent
all day at
the office
which unlike

her apartment was
air-conditioned &
as cold as the
morgue. There,
she said, I am
happy like an
opened up oyster
on a bed of ice.

Notes

The notes that follow cannot be comprehensive, nor is their intention to 'explain' the poems or disclose their secrets. Their purpose is twofold: to show the textual sources on which the present volume draws, and to throw light on some of Sebald's allusions to landscapes, works of art or literature, and other matters of historical interest. Points of reference and connotation inevitably inform a translator's decisions as he goes about the business of rebuilding a poem in a different language. Even following considerable effort of research, however, many details have remained obscure. Readers better acquainted than I am with the life and work of W. G. Sebald will recognize echoes, overtones and contexts that I may have overlooked.

In indicating the source of a poem, the following abbreviations will apply:

AK48 (*Akzente* 48 J.: 2001)

AK50 (*Akzente* 50 J.: 2003)

DK (*Der Komet. Almanach der Anderen Bibliothek auf das Jahr 1991*, Frankfurt am Main: 1991)

FL (Franz Loquai, *W. G. Sebald*, Eggingen: 1997)

FSZ (*Freiburger Studentenzeitung*)

FYN (Collection 'For Years Now', in: The Papers of W. G. Sebald, Deutsches Literaturarchiv, Marbach)

GG1 (File 'Gedichte und Gedichtentwürfe', Folder 1, in: The Papers of W. G. Sebald, Deutsches Literaturarchiv, Marbach)

H (Hanser Verlag volume *Über das Land und das Wasser*, ed. Sven Meyer, Munich: 2008)

JPT (Jan Peter Tripp, *Die Aufzählung der Schwierigkeiten: Arbeiten von 1985–92*, Offenburg: 1993)

K&C (*Konterbande und Camouflage. Szenen aus der Vor- und Nachgeschichte von Heinrich Heines marranischer Schreibweise*, Berlin: 2002)

NZZ (*Neue Zürcher Zeitung*, No. 256: 13 November 1999)

P (*Pretext*, Vol. 2: Autumn 2000)

PT (Collection 'Poemtrees. Lyrisches Lesebuch für Fortgeschrittene und Zurückgebliebene', Folders 1 & 2, in: The Papers of W. G. Sebald, Deutsches Literaturarchiv, Marbach)

SL (Folder 1: 'Schullatein', in Collection 'Über das Land und das Wasser', in: The Papers of W. G. Sebald, Deutsches Literaturarchiv, Marbach)

ÜLW (Folder 2: 'Über das Land und das Wasser', in Collection 'Über das Land und das Wasser', in: The Papers of W. G. Sebald, Deutsches Literaturarchiv, Marbach)

VVJ (Folder 3: 'Das vorvergange Jahr' in Collection 'Über das Land und das Wasser', in: The Papers of W. G. Sebald, Deutsches Literaturarchiv, Marbach)

WS (*Weltwoche Supplement*: Juni 1996)

ZET (*Das Zeichenheft für Literatur und Grafik*)

References to the works of W. G. Sebald in English are to the following volumes:

The Emigrants, trans. Michael Hulse, London: 1996

The Rings of Saturn, trans. Michael Hulse, London: 1998

Vertigo, trans. Michael Hulse, London: 1999

Austerlitz, trans. Anthea Bell, London: 2002

For Years Now, London: 2001

After Nature, trans. Michael Hamburger, London: 2002

On the Natural History of Destruction, trans. Anthea Bell, London: 2003

Unrecounted, trans. Michael Hamburger, London: 2004

Poemtrees

'For how hard it is'

PT, FSZ 14 (1964), H.

'A colony of allotments'

PT, FSZ 14 (1964), H.

'Smoke will stir'

PT, FSZ 14 (1964), H.

'The intention is sealed'

FSZ 14 (1964), H.

Nymphenburg

PT, FSZ 14 (1964), H.

Title: the gardens and interiors of the Baroque Nymphenburg Palace, formerly the summer residence of Bavaria's ruling Wittelsbach dynasty, are among Munich's most frequently visited attractions.

mauves: French for mallows.

Wishing Table: the poem invokes the Grimms' tales *'Dornröschen'* ('Sleeping Beauty', or 'Briar Rose') and *'Tischchen deck dich, Goldesel und Knüppel aus dem Sack'* ('The Wishing Table, the Gold Ass and the Cudgel in the Sack'), in which a table, on command, sets and spreads its own surface with food and drink.

Epitaph
FSZ 15 (1965), H.

Schattwald in Tyrol
PT, FSZ 15 (1965), H.

Title: Tyrolean village to the east of Oberjoch, from which the
narrator of the final section ('Il ritorno in patria') of Sebald's
Schwindel. Gefühle (1990; English trans. *Vertigo*, 1999) walks to
Wertach, the author's place of birth.

Rosetta Stone: an ancient Egyptian stele of black granodiorite,
inscribed with the so-called Memphis-decree, issued in three
languages in 196 BCE. Its discovery contributed to the
decipherment of Egyptian hieroglyphics. In an earlier version of
the poem the second stanza reads: 'Am Anfang der Legende /
brachte die Botschaft / der Engel des Herrn / ins Haus aus
Schatten' ('At the beginning of the legend / the Angel of the
Lord / brought the tidings / to the House of Shadows').

Remembered Triptych of a Journey from Brussels
PT, FSZ 15 (1965), H.

near Meran in Ezra's hanging garden: from 1958, after his release
from St Elizabeth's Hospital in Washington, DC, Ezra Pound
stayed at Castle Brunnenburg near Meran in northern Italy, the
home of his daughter Mary de Rachewiltz.

battlefield at Waterloo: Sebald's narrator describes visits to
Waterloo in the passage entitled (in the Contents) 'The
panorama of Waterloo' in the fifth chapter of *The Rings of
Saturn*, including a visit in December 1964 when he stayed at a
hotel near the Bois de la Cambre and visited a bar in Rhode-St-
Genèse.

Marie-Louises: young soldiers of the Napoleonic army in 1814, many of them fourteen to fifteen years old, who had been conscripted during the regency of Empress Marie-Louise, Napoleon's wife, during her husband's absence for the German campaign of 1813–14.

ferme in Genappe: the farmhouse was Napoleon's headquarters on the night of 17 June 1815, the eve of the Battle of Waterloo.

Marquise of O.: the reference to the eponymous protagonist of Heinrich von Kleist's story is obscure, but see note on *Light in August* below.

A woman's mouth . . . roses: in English in the German text.

Départ . . . Milan via St Gotthard: the train for Milan via St Gotthard departs from platform 8 at 00.16 hours.

industrie chimique: chemicals industry.

light above the heavenly vaults: in English in the German text.

Bahnhof von Metz: Metz train station.

bien éclairée: well illuminated.

Gregorius, the guote sündaere: 'Gregorius, the good sinner', a medieval verse epic by Hartmann von Aue (died *c.* 1210).

Au near Freiburg: one of the municipalities of that name which claim association with the poet.

rechtsrheinisch: on the right (eastern) side of the Rhine.

Froben & Company: the humanist Johann Froben (1460–1527), a friend of Erasmus of Rotterdam, set up a successful printing business in Basel in 1491.

Light in August: title of a novel (1932) by William Faulkner (1897–1962). One of the characters is Lena Grove, who, like the pregnant Marquise of O. in Heinrich von Kleist's story, mentioned earlier in the poem, is trying to find the father of her unborn child. To do so she walks a long distance to Jefferson, in *Yoknapatawpha*, the fictional setting of several of Faulkner's novels.

Life is Beautiful
PT, FSZ 15 (1965), H.

Matins for G.
PT, FSZ 15 (1965), H.

Where no kitchen / there no cook: as Leon, in Act I of Franz
   Grillparzer's drama *Weh dem, der lügt* ('Woe to Him Who Lies'),
   Vienna: 1840 (p. 6), exclaims: 'Wo keine Küche, ist kein Koch.'

Winter Poem
PT, FSZ 15 (1965), H.

Child Jesus in Flanders: the German translation of the Flemish writer
   Felix Timmermans's novel *Het Kindeken Jezus in Vlaanderen* (1917),
   published in 1919 under the title *Das Jesuskind in Flandern*, was
   immensely popular in Germany between the wars and during the
   1950s. Its plot sets the birth of Christ in rural Flanders. Another
   story, 'Jésus-Christ en Flandre' (1831) by Honoré de Balzac, is
   apparently based on a medieval folk tale. The Christ-child theme
   recalls the nativity scenes of Dutch Masters.

Believe and be saved: see Mark 16:16. A handwritten comment on
   the PT typescript claims there is too great a discrepancy in the
   poem between the ironic tone of the second stanza and the
   apparent naivety of the first.

Lines for an Album
PT, FSZ 15 (1965), H.

Bleston. A Mancunian Cantical
PT, H.

Title: in English in original text. Bleston is the name given to

Manchester in the 1956 novel *L'Emploi du temps* (translated into English as *Passing Time*) by the French writer Michel Butor (b. 1926). Like Sebald (from 1966 to 1968), Butor had been an assistant teacher at Manchester University (1951–3). The final section ('Max Ferber') of W. G. Sebald's prose work *The Emigrants* is set in Manchester, as is the fourth part of 'Dark Night Sallies Forth', the final section of *After Nature*. Sebald finished writing the poem on or shortly before 26 January 1967 (according to a letter he wrote to his friend Albrecht Rasche). The poem presents a labyrinth of allusions, and the reader who attempts to follow them risks becoming 'perdu dans ces filaments' ('lost in these filaments'), a fate of which the title of the fifth part of the poem appears to warn us.

I.

Fête nocturne: night-party.

II.

Consensus Omnium: agreement of all.
Place of / Breast-like hills: in English in the German text.
Dis Manibus . . . curavi: 'Dis manibus' is found on Roman gravestones, meaning 'for the spirits of the ancestors'; in this case, 'for the spirits of the ancestors I have arranged for the building of this Mamucium [Manchester]'.

III.

à traves les âges: through the ages.
Sharon's Full Gospel . . . Miraculously healed before our eyes: in English in the German text. According to the website stance of the Sharon Full Gospel Church, the Church 'began with a gospel mission in a tent in Pontypool Park during 1936. Many local

people were . . . miraculously healed.' There is a SFG church in South Manchester.

IV.

Lingua Mortua: dead language.

Kebad Kenya: character in an episode in the first volume (*Das Holzschiff*) of Hans Henny Jahnn's novel *Fluß ohne Ufer* (1949). The story has appeared in English in a translation by Gerda Jordan-Peterson in *The Ship* (1961) and *Thirteen Uncanny Stories* (1984). Briefly: Kebad decides to eat himself, fails to die, attempts to become one with his mare, lies down as if dead, is buried, witnesses the corruption of the flesh, is a revenant, takes possession of men's bodies, inflicts terror by stealing horses.

Hipasos [sic] *of Metapontum*: Pythagorean philosopher who conducted experiments in musical theory. Hippasos claimed the discovery of concords with bronze discs of equal diameter and varying thickness.

Et pulsae referunt ad sidera valles: and the valleys echoed the sounds to the stars (Virgil's *Eclogue* 6, l. 84).

fil d'Ariane: Ariadne's thread. The theme of Ariadne and Theseus, the labyrinth and Minotaur, are ever-present in Butor's novel *L'Emploi du temps*: 'that rope of words is like Ariadne's thread [*ce cordon des phrases est un fil d'Ariane*], because I am in a labyrinth, because I am writing in order to find my way about in it . . . the labyrinth of my days in Bleston, incomparably more bewildering than that of the Cretan palace, since it grows and alters even while I explore it' (*Passing Time*, trans. Jean Stewart, New York: 1969, p. 195).

opgekilte schottns: both words occur in the Yiddish lexicon, the second one more frequently as 'shotns'. If Sebald intended the words to be recognized as Yiddish, they would mean something like 'frozen shadows'. Perhaps they should be read in the context of return, albeit a return antithetical to the desired echo: the revenant murderous shadows of Kebad, or Theseus, who after abandoning Ariadne on Naxos forgot to change the black sail to white, thereby causing the death of his father, Aegeus.

Alma quies optata veni nam sic sine vita / Vivere quam suave est sic sine morte mori: 'How sweet, though lifeless, yet with life to lie, / And, without dying, O how sweet to die' (translation by John Walcott (1738–1813). Authorship of the epigram appears to be obscure, with Georg Christoph Lichtenberg attributing the lines to Heinrich Meibom (1555–1625), while British critics have tended to see the poet laureate Thomas Warton (1728–90) as the author.

Rapunzel: in the fairy-tale collected by the Brothers Grimm, Rapunzel, exiled to the wilderness by the witch to live on her own, one day hears the voice of the prince, whom the witch has blinded by throwing him from the tower. They reunite, his sight is restored, and they live happily ever after.

V.

Perdu dans ces filaments: lost in these filaments; a quotation from Michel Butor's novel *L'Emploi du temps* (Paris: 1956, p. 54; *Passing Time*, op. cit., p. 41): 'Thus I, a mere virus lost amidst its filaments, was able like a scientist armed with his microscope to study this huge cancerous growth.'

Eli Eli: Mark 15:34: 'Eloi, Eloi, lama sabachthani? ('My God, my God, why hast thou forsaken me?')

Mr Dewey's International classification system: Melville Louis Kossuth Dewey (1851–1931) invented a Decimal Classification System which revolutionized library cataloguing in the 1870s and 1880s.

On ne doit plus dormir: One must no longer sleep. The French dictum derives from Theodor W. Adorno's essay 'Commitment' (see *New Left Review*, First Series, No. 87–8, 1974, p. 85), first published in German in 1962: 'The abundance of real suffering tolerates no forgetting; Pascal's theological saying, *On ne doit plus dormir*, must be secularized.' Adorno, however, has adapted rather than cited Pascal, who wrote: 'Jésus sera en agonie jusqu'à la fin du monde. Il ne faut pas dormir pendant ce temps-là' ('The agony of Jesus will last until the world ends. Until that time, we must not sleep'), in: Blaise Pascal, *Pensées* (919) (Texte établi par Louis Lafuma), Paris: 1963 (p. 378).

Didsbury
PT, H.

Title: the author lived in Didsbury, a suburb of Manchester, from January 1967 until his departure in 1968 to teach at a school in St Gallen, Switzerland, initially sharing a flat with Reinbert Tabbert. The poem was among a small number of items, including 'Giulietta's Birthday' and 'Time Signal at Twelve', collected in a Festschrift put together in Summer 1967 by Reinbert Tabbert and Winfried Sebald (the name under which Sebald's poems appeared in the 1960s) for Idris Parry (1916–2008), Professor of German at the University of Manchester and Sebald's later supervisor for his MA dissertation (1968) on the German writer Carl Sternheim. An earlier version of the poem is entitled 'Weekend'.

Giulietta's Birthday
PT, H. See also note on 'Didsbury' above.

Time Signal at Twelve
PT, AK50. See also note on 'Didsbury' above.

Lejzer Ajchenrand: a Jewish poet born in Demblin (Poland) in 1911,

who emigrated to France in 1937 and served in a French
volunteer battalion. He was interned under the Vichy regime
and, in 1942, fled to Switzerland, where he was again interned.
Although Ajchenrand spent the rest of his life in Switzerland,
he was never granted Swiss citizenship. He died in the town of
Küsnacht, on Lake Zürich, Switzerland. His mother and sister
were murdered by the Nazis, and the Shoah remained the
subject of a poetic oeuvre composed entirely in Yiddish. Several
of his poems appeared in the German literary magazine *Akzente*.
The best-known of his nine books of poems is *Aus der Tiefe* ('De
Profundis'), first published in Paris in 1953, and reprinted with
German translations in 1998.

Melk: a town in Lower Austria and the site of a famous Benedictine
abbey, founded in 1089. Between April 1944 and May 1945,
14,390 mainly Jewish prisoners were deported to Melk
concentration camp, a sub-camp of KZ-Mauthausen. It is
thought that some 5,000 prisoners were murdered there. The
crematorium is all that remains of the camp today.

If no one asks him . . . knows not: the phrasing of the fifth stanza
echoes a passage in Augustine's *Confessiones* (XI, 14) in which
the author ruminates on the nature of time, its absence, and
eternity. 'Quid ergo tempus est?' ('What then is time?') he
asks, and continues, 'Si nemo ex me quaerat, scio; si quaerenti
explicare velim, nescio.' ('If no one asks me, I know; if I wish to
explain it to him who asks, I know not.')

Children's Song
PT, AK50.
The poem, dedicated to W. G. Sebald's niece, was first published in
Reinbert Tabbert's reminiscence of his friendship with Sebald in
the magazine *Akzente*. It later appeared in a second article by
Tabbert in a journal called *Literatur in Bayern* (No. 97: September

2009), this time with a short commentary linking the poem to the topography and mood of Sebald's childhood memories of his daily route to school in his native Wertach.

School Latin

Votive Tablet
SL.

Legacy
SL.

Sarassani
SL.
Title: Sebald's spelling may be incorrect, but only if the title refers to the Sarrasani Circus, founded by Hans Stosch (alias Giovanni Sarrasani) in Meißen in 1902, and still in family hands.

Day's Residue
PT, SL.
Title: a psychoanalytical term (German: 'Tagesrest') coined by Sigmund Freud in his book on the interpretation of dreams, *Die Traumdeutung* (1900). The term describes the way the residual material of a day's experience – thoughts, impressions and unfinished tasks – may trigger the 'dream work' of the following night.

Border Crosser
SL.
witch's thaler: a gold or silver coin whose currency magically alters

in accordance with the mint of the country in which its owner is resident.

Lay of Ill Luck
SL, H.

black bird: the combination of fox and crow (or, in German, 'Rabe', raven) is likely to be associated in the reader's mind with Aesop's ancient Greek fable 'The Fox and the Crow', or with its later French version by Jean de La Fontaine. However it is in Leoš Janáček's opera *The Cunning Little Vixen* (German: *Das schlaue Füchslein*; in Sebald's poem the fox is also a 'Füchslein') that the 'little vixen' escapes. The *monosyllabic creature* of the translation is, in German, 'einsilbig', which can also, figuratively at least, mean taciturn. 'Monosyllabic' at least captures Mistress Crow's 'Caw!', which lost her the cheese in the fable. The final stanza, however, may contain a nod to the taciturn 'black bird' in Edgar Allan Poe's poem 'The Raven', possibly a figure closer to Sebald's own melancholy muse.

Memorandum of the Divan
SL.

Il ritorno d'Ulisse
SL.

Title: probably a reference to Claudio Monteverdi's opera of 1640, whose full title is *Il ritorno d'Ulisse in patria*. The title of the final section ('Il ritorno in patria') of Sebald's prose work *Schwindel. Gelfühle* (1990; English trans. *Vertigo*) also appears to echo the title of Monteverdi's opera.

in scattered spots / with the black paper hearts of men / shot by the arquebuse: the German ('an zerstreueten Orten waren schwarze

Papierherzen arkebusierter Menschen') is from Jean Paul
Richter's novel *Titan* (Vol. I), in *Sämtliche Werke*, Bd. II, Berlin:
1827 (p. 115); translated into English by Charles T. Brooks as
'in scattered spots were the black paper hearts of men shot by
the arquebuse', in *Titan. A Romance*, London: 1863 (p. 36).

For a Northern Reader
SL.

Florean Exercise
SL.

Title: there is more than one reference in Sebald's work to the
name of the Northamptonshire village Flore. In the second
chapter of *The Rings of Saturn*, for example, the narrator's
neighbour, Frederick Farrar, is sent in 1914 to a prep school
near Flore in Northamptonshire. Flore is also mentioned in the
poem 'Pneumatological Prose' in this volume.

the Dardanian gods: the final lines cite an Etruscan inscription
discovered in North Africa by the French Latinist and Etruscan
scholar Jacques Heurgon.

Scythian Journey
SL.

Title: in classical antiquity Scythia was the area to the north of the
Black Sea and the Caspian Sea.

with the birds and fishes: reminiscent of lines in the second poem in
Book I of Horace's *Odes*: 'omne cum Proteus pecus egit altos
visera montis, / piscium et summa genus haesit ulmo, / nota
quae sedes fuerat columbis' ('when Proteus drove all his herd
to visit the high mountains / and the race of fishes lodged in the
elm-tops / which once were known as the haunt of doves').

Berecyntian horn: mentioned in Horace's *Odes*, Book I, 1. 18, but also to be found in Catullus, Ovid and other classical writers. Berecyntus was the name of a mountain in Phrygia, sacred to Cybele.

Penates: guardian deities of the household and state.

Saumur, selon Valéry

SL.

Title: Saumur, as seen by Valéry. There is a National Equestrian Academy at Saumur, home to the world-renowned 'Cadre Noir'. In his *Cahiers* ('Notebooks') the French poet Paul Valéry compares mental and aesthetic training with the equestrian art of dressage: he aims to write a treatise on 'le dressage de l'esprit' ('dressage of the mind'), to be called 'Gladiator'. In the *Cahiers* (VI, p. 901) he also mentions the mythical centaur as a model for perfect control. Another model was the Saumur equestrian instructor François Baucher (1796–1873), of whom Valéry, in his essay 'Autour de Corbot', relates an anecdote with which Sebald was evidently acquainted. Baucher dazzled one of his favourite pupils at Saumur by appearing as 'un centaure parfait' ('a perfect centaur'): 'Voilà . . . Je ne fais pas d'esbroufe. Je suis au sommet de mon art: *Marcher sans une faute*' ('There . . . I'm not showing off. I have reached the summit of my art: *Walking without error*'), in Paul Valéry, *Œuvres II*, Paris: 1960 (p. 1311).

L'instruction du roy

PT, SL, H.

Title: probably a reference to the posthumously published *L'Instruction du roy en l'exercise de monter à cheval* (1625) by Antoine de Pluvinel (1555–1620). The book was one of the earliest equestrian manuals and is conceived in the form of a conversation between the author, Louis XIII and Monsieur Le Grand, the King's Master of the Horse.

Festifal

PT.

the Dictaean Grotto: the 'Diktaion Andron' on Crete, traditionally the birthplace of Zeus.

polar dragon: according to Lemprière's classical dictionary this was the guardian of the apples of the Hesperides; see J. Lemprière, *Bibliotheca Classica*, London: 1811 (p. 340). As Ladon, the dragon is depicted coiling around the apple tree; in (ancient Egyptian) celestial atlases he is coiled around the pole of heaven. Could Sebald have been aware of W. B. Yeats's lines 'And though the Seven Lights bowed in their dance and wept, / The Polar Dragon slept, / His heavy rings uncoiled from glimmering deep to deep . . .' ('The Poet Pleads with the Elemental Powers')?

Somnia . . . Thessala: 'Somnia, terrores magicos, miracula, sagas, / nocturnos lemures portentaque Thessala rides?' are lines from the second book of Horace's *Epistles* (ll. 208–9), which Philip Francis, cited by Robert Burton in the *Anatomy of Melancholy*, translates as: 'Say, can you laugh indignant at the schemes / Of magic terrors, visionary dreams, / Portentous wonders, witching imps of Hell, / the nightly goblin, and enchanting spell?' See *The Works of the English Poets from Chaucer to Cowper*, Vol. VIII, London: 1810 (p. 742).

The plump Etruscan blows on an ivory flute in Virgil, *Georgics*, Book II, l. 193, trans. C. Day Lewis, Oxford: 1999 (p. 75).

Proteus: an ancient sea-god and herdsman of Poseidon's seal-herds.

The Sphinx fleeing toward Libya: 'I have seen the Sphinx fleeing toward Libya'; see *The Letters of Gustave Flaubert 1830–57*, ed. Francis Steegmuller, Cambridge, MA: 1980 (p. 112).

Pneumatological Prose

SL.

Flore: see note on 'Florean Exercise' above.

The animal is a victor: the indented passage is cited from the legend
in Dürer's 1515 woodcut of a rhinoceros. The passage in
Sebald's German text reads: 'Das da ein Sieg Thir ist / des
Heilffandten Todtfeindt / den wo es Ihn ankompt / so laufft
ihm das Thir mit dem Kopff / zwischen die fordern bayn / / Sie
sagen auch / das der Rhinocerus / schnellfraytig und auch
lustig sey'. The legend in Dürer's woodcut reads: 'das da ein
Sieg Thir ist / des Heilffandten Todtfeyndt. Der Heilffandt
fürchts fast ubel / den wo es Ihn ankompt / so laufft Ihm das
Thir mit dem kopff zwischen die fordern bayn / und reist den
Heilffanten unten am bauch auff / und er würget ihn / des mag
er sich nicht erwehren. dann das Thier ist also gewapnet / das
ihm der Jeilffandt nichts Thun kan / Sie sagen auch / das der
Rhinocerus / Schnell / fraytig / und auch Lustig / sey.'

as Pliny tells us: Pliny in Book VIII of the *Naturalis Historia* discusses
the character and virtues of the elephant. This passage recurs in
modified form in *Unrecounted* (p. 13).

Footnotes 1 and 2: the footnotes in the original text are reprinted
verbatim in the translation.

Messrs H. and C. Artmann: a pun on the name of the Viennese poet
H. C. Artmann (1921–2000).

Comic Opera

SL.

Title: comic opera ('komische Oper') can be opera buffa, with its
beginnings in the Italian eighteenth century, or the often more
serious, or satirical, opéra comique.

green theatre: 'théâtre de verdure', a garden or hedge theatre.

Timetable

ZET, SL, H.

Cretan trick: an acrobatic feat of bull-leaping or somersaulting over or between a bull's horns. Depictions of the ritual, possibly once a rite of passage for young men, have been found in ancient Minoan artwork.

Unexplored

ZET, SL, H.

Title: 'Unexplored', as a title, suggests the white areas once representing unexplored regions in old maps.

horoscope, heptagram, malefic houses: Sebald returns again and again to magic, astrology, alchemy, etc.

photoset: a development in typesetting allowing characters to be projected onto film for offset printing. The technique had its heyday in the 1960s, when the poem was probably written. The technique may have been state-of-the-art, and yet the 'malefic houses' were still ignored (unexplored). In an earlier version of the poem the 'evil houses' have been whited out, replaced by 'white zones' in the school historical atlas.

Elizabethan

PT, SL, ÜLW, ZET, H.

a baker's daughter: see *Hamlet*, Act IV, Scene 5, Ophelia: 'They say the owl was a baker's daughter. Lord, we know what we are, but know not what we may be.'

Sheikh Subir: doubts about Shakespeare's authorship of the plays are recurrent. In one version it was claimed, apparently by the nineteenth-century Lebanese writer and scholar Ahmad Faris al-Shidyaq (1804–87), that 'Shakespeare' was an Arab called Sheykh

Zubayr (see Muhammad Mustafá Badawī, *Modern Arabic Literature*, London: 1985, p. 191).

Baroque Psalter
SL.

One of several 'found' poems by W. G. Sebald, this is taken almost
  verbatim from a review by Heinz Ludwig Arnold, in *Die Zeit*
  (30 June 1972), of the Baroque poet Quirinus Kuhlmann's
  (1651–89) so-called *Kühlpsalter* of 1684: 'Nach zahlreichen
  Bekehrungsreisen nach Paris, Genf, Smyrna und Konstantinopel
  wurde Kuhlmann in Moskau als politischer Aufrührer
  verbrannt.'

Across the Land and the Water

Cold Draught
PT, ÜLW, H.

Title: the German 'Zug' can mean, among other things, a train, a
  draft in the sense of an outline or sketch, the action of drawing
  air, smoke or liquid, or a current of air. The poem describes a
  train journey, but the primary sense of the title is probably the
  icy cultural draught that blows through the narrator's
  sensibility as he returns to the scenes of his childhood and
  place of origin. Sebald's landscapes are never innocent.
  Landsberg housed the headquarters of the Kaufering complex of
  eleven concentration camps, the largest such complex within
  Germany itself, and was itself the site of KZ-Außenlage
  Kaufering I. *Kaufbeuren* was the site of a psychiatric hospital in
  which the mentally ill were murdered under the Nazi
  euthanasia programme. Between 1939 and 1945 some 2,000

patients from Kaufbeuren and the nearby Irsee Abbey were deported to their deaths. The Riederloh II camp housed forced labourers who worked at the DAG munitions factory in Kaufbeuren. Landsberg is also significant for its prison, where Hitler was incarcerated and allegedly wrote *Mein Kampf*, and where 275 Nazi war criminals were executed between 1945 and 1951.

Saint Elizabeth: could Sebald have been mistaken? It was not St Elizabeth but St Kunigunde of Luxemburg – whose husband was Heinrich II and the last Holy Roman Emperor of the Ottonian Dynasty – who walked over red-hot ploughshares unscathed to prove her innocence. Her veil, according to another legend, was said to have prevented the Allies from successfully bombing Bamberg, where Kunigunde was buried in 1040.

Near Crailsheim
ÜLW.

Title: to set an example the Americans razed Crailsheim to the ground at the end of the war. The town suffered some 90 per cent damage as a result of the bombing after the Germans had successfully retaken it from the Americans in a battle in April 1945. After its destruction the town was not rebuilt according to historical principles (as was often the case in German restoration) but employing architectural ideas of the 1940s. The descriptions of landscape in the poem exude Sebald's antipathy for what he would later describe (e.g. in the description of a train journey in the last chapter of *Vertigo*, or *passim* in *On the Natural History of Destruction*) as a repressive German tidiness during the post-war decades, an outward reversal of moral devastation, the avoidance of memory, and the inability to mourn.

Jehoshaphat: Hebrew, meaning 'Jehovah has judged'. For the 'valley of *Jehoshaphat*', see Joel:3, especially verses 2 and 19. The valley, also mentioned in the final section of *After Nature* (p. 90), is referred to as the 'valley of decision' (Joel 3:14). It is where the Lord assembled those who had afflicted Judah, and wreaked upon them his judgement.

Poor Summer in Franconia

ÜLW.

Colorado beetle: by 1936 the westward spread of the Colorado potato beetle through continental Europe had reached Germany, destroying crops as it went. Widespread infestation continued until the 1950s.

Five lines of the poem are incorporated into the final section of *After Nature* (p. 89).

Solnhofen

ÜLW.

Title: a small town in Franconia (a region of Bavaria).

winged vertebrates of prehistory: the Solnhofen limestone *lagerstätte* (sedimentary deposit) has supplied some of the most significant fossils ever found, including the Jurassic Archaeopteryx, the so-called *Urvogel*, or 'first bird'. See also the first lines of 'Dark Night Sallies Forth', in *After Nature* (p. 81).

Leaving Bavaria

ÜLW, H.

a Reichspost stamp . . . Hindenburg's grey-green millions: by November 1923 hyperinflation had rendered the German Reichsmark valueless, and postage stamps had to be overprinted daily with surcharges of up to 10 billion marks.

null ouvert: the term derives from the popular German card game

'Skat'. 'Null ouvert' is the only game where the 'Declarer' wins
if he manages to lose every trick.

gondola: the term for the cabin of an airship.

Saint Dionysius: the patron saint of Paris, St Denis, whose tradition
and martyrdom involve his carrying his head under one arm, is
known in German as St Dionysius. There is a statue
commemorating St Dionysius in Bamberg cathedral, probably
because Pope Clemens II, who is buried there, died on St
Dénis' commemoration day.

Something in My Ear
SL, ÜLW, H.

Panacea
SL, ZET, ÜLW, H.

Much of this poem occurs in the second section of 'Dark Night
Sallies Forth' in *After Nature* (p. 88).

Mithraic
SL, ZET, ÜLW, H.

Title: Mithra was a Zoroastrian divinity of the oath.

Zarvan: the Zoroastrian time-father creator, the father too of
Ahriman and Ormuzd, recurring figures in Sebald's work.
The Zurvanist creation myth holds that Zurvan, or Zarvan,
promised to sacrifice, or pray, for a thousand years for
descendants (who would then be able to create everything in
the world). Before the period was finished, however, he began
to have doubts that his wishes would be fulfilled, and at that
moment he conceived the twins Ahriman (for doubt) and
Ormuzd (for sacrifice).

sea-goat: this is Capricorn, created when Pan leaped into the sea to

escape the Titan Typhon, growing a fish's tail as he did so. The
sea-goat is a symbol of renewed vitality and new beginnings.

world egg: the oldest world-egg myth, a symbol for the beginning
of all things, goes back to the Sanskrit scriptures.

Memo
SL, ZET, ÜLW, H.

Barometer Reading
SL, ÜLW, H.

ignoring their ladders: weather-frogs (tree-frogs) were kept in
preserve glasses with some water in the bottom and a small
ladder. If the weather was changing for the better the frog
would climb the ladder; if rain was imminent the frog
descended the ladder.

Propertius: Sextus Propertius, Latin poet (*c.* 50–15 BCE). In Book
III.3 of his *Elegies*, Phoebus advises the poet: 'Why have your
pages left their set course? / Do not overload the boat of your
skill. / With one oar skim the water, with the other the sand. /
You will be safe: the storm is out at sea' (my translation).

K.'s Emigration
SL, ZET, ÜLW, H.

Bohemian Switzerland, the *High Tatras* and *Franzensbad* are all places
frequented by Kafka. The final stanza cites a postcard, written
by Kafka (dated June 1921) from Matliary in the High Tatras, to
his parents, who were taking a *Kur* ('cure') in Franzensbad. The
postcard picture shows Kafka surrounded by fellow patients
and staff. The *you* and *your* – at least in the context of Kafka's
postcard – addresses Kafka's parents.

Through Holland in the Dark
PT, ÜLW, H.

Kaiser Wilhelm II, sometimes referred to colloquially as 'Kaiser Willem', abdicated as German Emperor and King of Prussia in November 1918 and went into exile in the Netherlands, where he lived in the town of Doorn until his death in 1941. The 'Willem II' brand of cigars, however, was named after Prince William II of Orange (1626–50).

Abandoned
ÜLW.

Goethe's abominable nature: entry for 31 January 1912 in Kafka's diary: 'Wrote nothing. Weltsch brings books on Goethe that leave me in a distracted and useless state of excitement. Plan for an essay: "Goethe's Abominable Nature". Fear of the two-hour walk I've started taking in the evenings' (my translation).

Mölkerbastei
SL, ZET, ÜLW, H.

Title: Beethoven lived in the Pasqualati House, at Mölkerbastei 8 in Vienna.

polished: a pun is lost in translation; the German has 'gewienert', 'polished', which contains the word 'wienern', to speak with a Viennese accent.

chair: Beethoven sat at the piano in a chair, not on a piano stool. From the *tidy* room, through the missing *chair* to the *proviso*, it is clear the museum must not be disturbed. History must be kept tidy. Beethoven is allowed in at night – provided his compositions are more or less inaudible.

A Galley Lies off Helsingborg
ÜLW.

Title: ('Liegt eine Galeere bei Helsingborg') Sebald is quoting a quotation; Heinrich von Kleist cites an entry from No. 997 of the 'Privilegierte Liste der Börsen-Halle' (12 October 1810) in his curious article entitled 'Miscellen' (varia), published in the *Berliner Abendblätter* (15 October 1810), a daily newspaper of which he was editor. One of three short entries in the 'Miscellen' ran as follows: 'Se. Hoheit der Kronprinz von Schweden ist in Hamburg angekommen, und es liegt eine Galleere [sic] bei Helsingborg, um ihn zugleich bei der Überfahrt zu begrüßen' ('His Highness the Crown Prince of Sweden has arrived in Hamburg, and a galley lies off Helsingborg to welcome him when he crosses'). Kleist's reduction to contextual absurdity of a detail gleaned from the official listings of a Hamburg newspaper had satirical intent. See also Roland Borgards, 'Experimentelle Aeronautik. Chemie, Meteorologie und Kleists Luftschiffkunst in den "Berliner Abendblättern"', in *Kleist-Jahrbuch 2005*, eds. Günter Bamberger und Ingo Breuer, Stuttgart: 2005 (p. 156). The port of Helsingborg in Sweden faces the Danish town of Helsingör, the Elsinore of Shakespeare's *Hamlet*, across the Öresund Strait.

Holkham Gap
PT, SL, ÜLW, H.

Title: on the Norfolk coast between Blakeney Point and Wells-next-the-Sea.

sea lion: Operation Sea Lion (1940), Hitler's only serious plan for the invasion of Britain, which, however, following British success in the Battle of Britain, was continually postponed.

Uncle Toby wishes for war in Chapter XXXII of Book 6 of Laurence
   Sterne's *Tristram Shandy*.

Norfolk
SL, ZET, ÜLW, H.
The physical (or rather metaphysical) attitude of the passenger,
   who is *sailing backwards . . . with banished time*, is reminiscent of
   Walter Benjamin's 'angel of history': the 'storm [from
   Paradise] irresistibly propels him into the future to which his
   back is turned, while the pile of debris before him grows
   skyward' (*Illuminations*, trans. Harry Zohn, London: 1973 (p.
   260)).
Louisianian: the reason for the poem's description of Norfolk as a
   'Louisianian' landscape is obscure. If the adjective refers to the
   US state of Louisiana the comparison is not entirely
   unfounded: the American state has some 6,000 miles of
   navigable waterways, including 3,000 miles of canals, while
   the 1961 edition of the *Encyclopaedia Britannica* (published
   some five to ten years before the poem was written) states
   that the 'low regions' of Louisiana, consisting largely of
   alluvial lands and reclaimable swampland, make up half of the
   entire state.
Egyptian: many years after the poem was written, the narrator in
   Chapter 4 of Sebald's East Anglian peregrination *The Rings of
   Saturn* would remember Denis Diderot's description of Holland
   as 'the Egypt of Europe', where one could sail through the
   fields in a boat. Perhaps Sebald had in mind the renowned
   Norfolk 'wherry' *Hathor*, designed in 1905 using Egyptian
   hieroglyphics and mythological images. Norfolk wherries, of
   which only half a dozen survive today, may be said to resemble
   Egyptian feluccas.

Crossing the Water
ÜLW.

The poem, with the exception of the date, is almost identical to
lines at the end of Section I of 'Dark Night Sallies Forth' in
After Nature (p. 85). In Michael Hamburger's translation the
passage reads: 'and a little later, / crossing to Floridsdorf / on
the Bridge of Peace, / I nearly went out of my mind.' The
German (in *Nach der Natur*) is: 'und wenig später hätte ich /
bei einem Gang über / die Friedensbrücke fast / den Verstand
verloren', *Nach der Natur*, Frankfurt am Main: 2004 (first publ.
1988) (p. 75). Did Sebald ask Michael Hamburger to insert
Floridsdorf? Interestingly, various bridges do cross the Donau
to Floridsdorf, but the Friedensbrücke (Bridge of Peace),
which crosses the Donau-Kanal more or less from the Franz-
Josefs-Bahnhof in Alsergrund to Brigittenau, is not one of
them.

Natural History
SL, ÜLW.

Title: in English in the original text.

Another of Sebald's 'found' poems, taken verbatim from Johann
Wilhelm Ritter's *Fragmente aus dem Nachlaß eines jungen
Physikers*, Bd. 2, Heidelberg: 1810 (p. 61) – see also note on
'Trigonometry of the Spheres' below. Ritter explains the
position of Man in relation to the other 'quarters' of the
world: birds, worms, fishes, insects. Man is at the centre of a
cross formed by the intersection of lines joining these four
regions of being. However ironic, Sebald's use of the 'found'
material illustrates the continuity of his fascination for matters
arcane, alchemical and astrological.

Ballad

PT, SL, ÜLW, H.

Title: 'Ballad' refers less to the poetic genre of Sebald's poem than
   to the preferred form of its subject's compositions. *Carl Löwe*, or
   Carl Loewe, is known to have set several hundred ballads to
   music. The poem is an exercise in negotiating the Uncertainty
   Principle. It all seems simple – or even slight – at first, but the
   choice of words, the order in which they appear, and the
   question form itself, allow for a baffling range of variables. Is
   Carl Löwe's (or Loewe's) heart (or is it in fact his liver, or
   tongue, or indeed somebody else's heart?) really immured (or
   has it been hung or buried?) in a column (or is it the pulpit?) of
   St Jacob's Church, or the Jacobus or Jacobi Church, or the
   Church of St James, or the Cathedral Basilica of St James the
   Apostle in Stettin, or, more politically correct, in Szczecin? Well,
   is it? Go and see (if you can see through stone, that is). If you
   can't find the heart where the poem suggests it is, you might try
   searching for a recess in the great C-pipe of the organ. Carl
   Loewe was the church organist at St James's for forty-six years.

Obscure Passage

SL, ÜLW, H.

did not apprehend . . . the word: readers who – as I have attempted to do
   and failed – wish to identify the source of misunderstanding or
   incomprehension the poem refers to may find it useful to know
   that 'Wort' – here translated as *word* – can also mean dictum or
   expression. It need not therefore be merely a single word we are
   looking for. Perhaps understanding itself is the key. In German
   'verstehen' not only stands for the cognitive process, but may
   denote the physical act of comprehension, symbolically and

actually located, at least partly, in the faculty of hearing. *Archytas* of
Tarentum, who was active in the third century BCE, was one of the
first and most influential classical proponents of a theory of the
limitations of hearing. Archytas maintained, for example, that
harmony might be developed far beyond our limited physical
apprehension of sound, and that its ultimate understanding cannot
therefore be attained via our senses: 'for the great sounds do not
steal into our hearing, just as nothing is poured into narrow-
mouthed vessels, whenever someone pours a lot'. See Carl A.
Huffman, *Archytas of Tarentum*, Cambridge: 2005 (p. 107).

Poetry for an Album
ÜLW, H.

The first stanza appears in different versions in Sebald's volumes *For
Years Now* (p. 48) and *Unrecounted* (p. 23). It consists largely of a
quotation from Jean Paul's novel *Flegeljahre* ('Uncouth Youth'). See
Jean Pauls Sämtliche Werke, XXVI, Berlin: 1827 (p. 61): 'Gefühle,
sagt' er, sind Sterne, die bloß bei hellem Himmel leiten, aber die
Vernunft ist eine Magnetnadel, die das Schiff noch ferner führt,
wenn jene auch verborgen sind und nicht mehr leuchten'
('Feelings, he said, are stars which guide us only when the sky is
clear; but reason is the needle that carries on guiding the ship even
when the former are hidden and no longer shine out').

palsied: Schumann suffered from digital paralysis. A revised version
of the fourth stanza appears in *After Nature*, at the beginning of
the third section of 'Dark Night Sallies Forth' (p. 91).

Carnaval (with this spelling) is a piano work (Op. 9) by Schumann.

For *Ormuzd and Ariman*, see note on 'Mithraic' above. The
conventional spelling is Ahriman.

whistling sound: a slightly different version of these lines is found in
For Years Now (p. 75).

Eerie Effects of the Hell Valley Wind on My Nerves
ÜLW, H.

Title: the Höllentäler, translated here as *Hell Valley Wind*, is an
evening wind in Freiburg (where Sebald studied), blowing from
East to West through the Höllental and Dreisam valley. In a
different context, perhaps, the word 'Höllental' need not have
been translated, but the poem requires the reader's alertness to
a notion of human hell – the world of *Daniel Paul Schreber*.
Schreber was a presiding judge in Dresden who was admitted
to an asylum at the height of his career and believed God was
turning him into a woman. Freud wrote on his case, as did
Jung, Elias Canetti, Gilles Deleuze and Jacques Lacan. Schreber
wrote accounts (*Memoirs of My Nervous Illness*) of his various
periods of treatment in asylums. In one, it is clear that some of
his oppressors and the malevolent changes they made in the
world were linked to *Cassiopeia*. The phrase *Order of the World* is
a quotation from Daniel Paul Schreber's memoirs.

li più reconditi principii della naturale filosofia: 'the most secret
principles of natural philosophy'; from *Prodomo* (1670) by
Francesco Lana di Terzi (1631–87), a Jesuit who proposed the
idea of a vacuum airship and invented an early form of Braille.

stony guest: in his memoirs Schreber describes himself as a 'stony
guest' who has returned from the distant past to a world grown
unfamiliar.

Open . . . into hell: the final stanza is in English in the original text.

Unidentified Flying Objects
ÜLW.

Title: in English in the original text.

lake of Idwal: Llyn Idwal, a small lake overshadowed by the Glyders at the head of Ogwen Valley in Snowdonia. According to legend the *Welsh prince* Idwal, a son of Owain Gwynedd, was murdered there.

The Sky at Night
ÜLW.

Title: in English in the original text.

A Peaceable Kingdom
ÜLW.

Title: in English in the original text. A number of works by the Quaker 'naive' artist Edward Hicks (1780–1849) were known as the *Peaceable Kingdom* paintings, and based on Isaiah 11:6: 'The wolf also shall dwell with the lamb, and the leopard shall lie down with the kid; and the calf and the young lion and the fatling together; and a little child shall lead them.' The paintings are reminiscent of the 'Paradise Landscape' works of Jan Brueghel; see also note below on the final poem in the 'The Year before Last' section, 'In the Paradise Landscape'. Parts of the text derive from the abecedarian 'Shaker Manifesto' of 1882, republished as a pre-school text in 1981 under the title *A Peaceable Kingdom: The Shaker Abecedarius,* illustrated by Alice and Martin Provensen.

Crocodile . . . bear: original text in English.

Are these . . . our love: original text in English.

Trigonometry of the Spheres
ÜLW, H.

the moon is the earth's work of art: 'Der Mond ist ein Kunstwerk der Erde' is cited from Johann Wilhelm Ritter's *Fragmente aus dem Nachlaß eines jungen Physikers*, op. cit. (p. 142), where we also

read 'Der Mond ist ein Thier' ('the moon is an animal'). See
also note for 'Natural History' above.

The notion that a *holy man* sits 'where night turns to day' ('wo die
Nacht sich wendet') is adapted from the Talmud (Berachot 3a),
whose German translation writes not of 'ein Heiliger' ('*a* holy
man') but of 'der Heilige': 'At every watch the Holy-One-
Blessed-Be-He sits and roars like a lion.'

Day Return
ÜLW, H.

Title: original text in English.

tatzelwurm: fabled Alpine dragon with long snake-like body.

the Hunter Gracchus: the title of a story-fragment by Franz Kafka.
Gracchus, after his death, remains perpetually trapped between
life and death, travelling from place to place in a small boat in
search of the 'beyond', occasionally going ashore but never
finding what he is looking for, in a state of permanent exile.
Gracchus is a recurrent figure in Sebald's work, and especially
prominent in *Vertigo*.

Hands off Caroline: original text in English.

Who knows the noises . . . whistle a new song: original text in English.

People taking to boats . . . Windsor Park: original text in English.

Baybrooke: Sebald has dropped an 'r'; the incident described in
Pepys's Diary concerns Bishop Braybrooke. This passage is
not cited directly from the Diary for 1666 but appears to be
taken from an entry in the *Index Volume*, edited by Robert
Latham, of *The Diary of Samuel Pepys*, XI, Berkeley, CA: 1983
(p. 105). The scene, pulling out of Liverpool Street Station
while reading Samuel Pepys's Diary, recurs in the final pages
of *Vertigo*.

New Jersey Journey
ÜLW, H.

Title: in English in the original text.

Several passages here later return in *The Emigrants*, in the chapter 'Ambros Adelwarth', in which a visit to the narrator's uncle Kasimir in the Lakehurst and Dover Beaches area is similarly described. See *The Emigrants* (pp. 72–3, 80–81 and 88–9). The third stanza is echoed in Part IV of 'Dark Night Sallies Forth', the final section of *After Nature* (p. 97).

The Year before Last

The Year before Last
DK, H.

Some parallels (the motor-cyclist, the 'firs growing all the way down to the outlying houses' (here *Black spruces thronged / to the edge of the outer buildings*), the white-haired waiter bringing 'Cuban cigarettes') may be found in Sebald's prose work *Austerlitz* (pp. 290–92, 299–300). It might therefore be inferred that these details travelled from the poem to the later prose work. While this may indeed be the case, the common ancestor of both works is undoubtedly a chapter entitled 'Marienbad' in Heinrich Laube's *Reisenovellen* ('Travel Novellas'), Vol. I, Leipzig: 1834 (pp. 426–38). Several passages and identical turns of phrase as well as scenic structuring in Laube's text are cited in the present poem, references that reveal the former's significance as a subtext (including foreshadowing of the themes of anti-Semitism and the Marie-character) for the Marienbad-episode in *Austerlitz*. 'The Year before Last' contains a number of further references and quotations:

pertrified magical city: from Novalis, *Schriften*, Berlin: 1837 (p. 149).

Is not the world here still . . . upon the cliffs? Johann Wolfgang von
  Goethe, 'Marienbader Elegie', in *Gedichte und Epen*, Band I,
  Hamburger Ausgabe, Munich: 1981/1996 (p. 382).
Rabbi of Belz: in letters to Max Brod (17/18 July 1916) and to
  Felix Weltsch (19 July 1916) Franz Kafka described his
  impressions of the Belzer Rabbi and his entourage.
The match game . . . an inch closer: Alain Robbe-Grillet (screen-
  writer) and Alain Resnais (director), *L'Année dernière à Marienbad*
  (*Last Year at Marienbad*), 1961: various scenes.
I am wholly yours ('ich bin ganz dein'): Goethe wrote such words
  on several occasions (to Charlotte von Stein: November 1783
  and 26 January 1786; to Christiane Vulpius: 25 August 1792),
  but a more likely source is the performance of a play entitled
  Rosmer – possibly a reference to Ibsen's *Rosmersholm* (1886),
  among whose characters are Rosmer and Rebecca – at the
  beginning of *L'Année dernière à Marienbad*, which closes with the
  (play's) character Rebekka's words 'Voilà . . . maintenant . . . je
  suis à vous' ('That's it . . . now . . . I am yours'), after which,
  however, she does not move 'an inch closer' to Rosmer.
the corridors . . . crimson tapestry: Friedrich Schiller, *Wallenstein's
  Death* (Act Five, Scene 11).

A Waltz Dream
JPT, H.

Title: Ein Walzertraum (*A Waltz Dream*) was one of Oscar Strauss's
  many operettas in the popular Viennese style. Completed in
  1907, it was composed to a libretto by Felix Dörmann and
  Leopold Jacobson, who based their work on Hans Müller's *Das
  Buch der Abenteuer*. Strauss adapted the score for *The Smiling
  Lieutenant*, a 1931 Hollywood film. The title of Jan Peter Tripp's
  picture of 1990 is *The Land of Smiles*, a reference to Franz
  Lehár's operetta, *Das Land des Lächelns*. Tripp, who lives in the

Alsace region of France, had been Sebald's friend since their schooldays in Oberstdorf in the early 1960s. They collaborated on the volume *Unrecounted*, and Sebald published a study of Tripp's work in his volume of essays *Logis in einem Landhaus* ('A House in the Country'), 1998. The essay – 'As Day and Night, Chalk and Cheese: On the Pictures of Jan Peter Tripp' – is included in Michael Hamburger's English translation of *Unrecounted* (pp. 78–94).

Dr Tulp is the surgeon at the centre of Rembrandt's painting *The Anatomy Lesson of Dr Nicolaes Tulp* (1632). The painting is reproduced in Sebald's *The Rings of Saturn*.

Donderdag

GG1.

Title: the events referred to in 'Donderdag', the activities of the notorious 'Bende van Venlo' (the 'Venlo gang'), were reported in various newspapers in the Netherlands in February 1995 and later at their trial. The passages in Dutch are quotations from a report by Hans Moleman in the *Volkskrant* (23 February 1995).

& *Frankfurt*: from approximately 1995 – in a process completed by 1999 – Sebald's poems tend to prefer the ampersand to the more conventional conjunction 'and'. In these final years of his life, as a writer frequently invited to readings and other literary events, Sebald would sometimes jot down first drafts of his poems 'on the road' – on menus or hotel stationery. In his subsequent fair copies, however, the author generally retained the shorthand ampersand – apparently (and his penchant for the short, two-stressed line may be another instance of this) adapting poetic form to a life of passing 'in a train / from here to there', across the land and the water.

Translations of passages in Dutch:

Donderdag: Thursday.

canavalsmoorden / van Venlo: the Venlo carnival murders.

koffieshop branche: coffee-bar business.

twee oude mensen / met doorgesneden / keel op de grund: two old
people with their throats cut, lying on the ground.

Turkse / gemeenschap & / Duitse clientèle: Turkish community and
German clients.

*een zwarte Merce / des een rode BMW / & twee kogels van / dichtbij in
het hoofd*: a black Mercedes, a red BMW and two bullets in the
head fired at close range.

The secrets
GG1.

From a manuscript handwritten on the headed notepaper of the
Hotel Schweizerhof in the Hinüberstraße, Hannover. See also
'Room 645' below.

On 9 June 1904
VVJ, WS, H.

Title: on 3 June 1904 the Russian dramatist and short-story writer
Anton Pavlovich Chekhov, suffering from tuberculosis, set off
with his wife Olga Leonardovna Knipper-Chekhova to the
Black Forest spa resort of Badenweiler, where he died on 1 July
by the Julian calendar, on 15 July by our own. Many of the
details in the poem can be gleaned from Chekhov's letters, in
the final two weeks of his life, from Badenweiler to his sister, or
from his wife's memoir.

Ninety years later
VVJ, WS, H.

Badenweiler: see note above.

In Bamberg

VVJ, FL, H.

the Little Hunchback: ('das bucklige Männlein') a figure from the
collection of folk poetry entitled *Des Knaben Wunderhorn* (1805–
8), collected by Clemens Brentano and Achim Arnim.

Empress Kunigunde . . . Katzenberg: see note for 'Cold Draught' above.

the dog Berganza: a talking dog in E. T. A. Hoffmann's story
'Nachricht von den neuesten Schicksalen des Hundes Berganza'
('Report on the New Adventures of the Dog Berganza'),
written in 1814–15, set in Bamberg, and based on Cervantes's
'Dialogue of the Dogs' (1613). Hoffmann lived in Bamberg
from 1808 to 1813, and the story starts with the narrator, who
has just crossed the river, meeting the talking dog in what is
apparently the *Hain park*, Bamberg's oldest park.

Schorsch and Rosa: Georg Sebald and Rosa, or Rosi, Egelhofer, the
poet's parents. The scene is probably based on the same
photograph described in the first section of 'Dark Night Sallies
Forth' in *After Nature* (p. 83).

Kara Ben Nemsi: fictional character and 'cowboy of the Orient' in
the works of the highly popular nineteenth-century German
children's writer Karl May.

Marienbad Elegy

VVJ, NZZ, H.

Title: like Wolfgang von Goethe's 'Marienbad Elegy', from his
'Trilogy of Passion' sequence of 1823, Sebald's poem consists of
twenty-three six-line stanzas, and one might think any
resemblance to Goethe's metrically controlled rhyming 'tempest
of feeling' ended there, were it not for the title. Sebald's
detachment from the 'Dichterfürst' (prince of poets) is respectful
in the mildness of its irony, and yet one senses that something
about Ulrike's personal effects, preserved in the Marienbad

Museum, must have touched the twentieth-century author and inspired him to write his own pensive elegy. The apparent subject of the poem is Goethe's unrequited love, at the age of seventy-three, for the eighteen-year-old Ulrike von Levetzow, whom he had met at Marienbad a year earlier, and would see for the last time a year later in Karlsbad, on the occasion of his seventy-fourth birthday. Ulrike remained a spinster, and died in 1899 at the age of ninety-five. The poet Michael Hamburger, who made a translation of 'Marienbad Elegy' not long after W. G. Sebald's death, has written that Ulrike von Levetzow died 'a full century and a half after her rejected lover's birth. Somehow this almost macabre time-span strikes me as relevant to the irony and pathos of a poem obsessed as its author was with transitoriness and the interweaving of seemingly unconnected phenomena and events.' See *Irish Pages*, Autumn/Winter 2002/2003 (p. 132).

At the edge
VVJ, H.
This poem and the three that follow, from the ambit of what Sebald called his 'micropoems', were not included in the volumes *For Years Now* or *Unrecounted*.

And always
GG1. See note above.

How silvery
GG1. See note for 'At the edge'.

Somewhere
GG1. See note for 'At the edge'.
Türkenfeld is a small town on the Allgäubahn (Allgäu Railway). A brief

discussion of the significance of Türkenfeld and its surrounding region during the period of National Socialism appears in the 'Translator's Introduction' prefacing this volume (see pp. xx–xxii). Sources: *Augenzeugen und Bilder berichten. Die Häftlinge aus den KZ-Außenlagern Landsberg/Kaufering auf dem Todesmarsch im April 1945 durch den Landkreis Fürstenfeldbruck nach Dachau*: Arbeitskreis Mahnmal Fürstenfeldbrück, Fürstenfeldbrück, 2007; 'Berichte von Zeitzeugen aus der Hölle von Kaufering', in: *The European Holocaust Memorial: Bürgervereinigung Landsberg im 20. Jahrhundert e.V.* (www.buergervereinigung-landsberg.org).

In the sleepless
VVJ, AK48, H.

Town Musicians: the Grimms' tale of the 'Town Musicians of Bremen' about a donkey, cat, dog and cockerel who attack a robber in the dark.

Room 645
VVJ, AK48, H.

My ICE Rail-Planner
VVJ, AK48, H.

The poem appears to contain a collage of so-called 'found' material, elements of which – e. g. text from hoardings, advertisements or passages from newspaper articles – Sebald frequently integrated into his poems. See, for other examples, the notes on 'Baroque Psalter', 'Natural History' or 'Donderdag'.

radio, transmission . . . building components: advertisement by Alcatel Sel AG in the *Berliner Zeitung*, 'Wirtschaft' (19 November 1994).

One Sunday in Autumn 94
VVJ, AK48, H.

Father of the German Nation: casts Helmut Kohl, the first German chancellor after German Reunification, in the role of the 'Iron Chancellor', Otto von Bismarck.

Calm November weather
VVJ, AK48, H.

literary villa: founded by Walter Höllerer in 1963 and one of the most important literary institutions in Berlin, indeed in Germany; the Literarisches Colloquium Berlin hosts a constant flow of readings, seminars and discussions throughout the year and also functions as a guesthouse for writers-in-residence. Sebald visited the Colloquium on several occasions. On one such occasion, in November 1997, the Greenlandic poet Jessie Kleemann read from her work.

Unchanged for years
VVJ, AK48, H.

The list of common brand names in the second stanza (*Nordhäuser Doppelkorn* is a spirit, *Gau Köngernheimer Vogelsang* a wine from the Rheinhessen region, and *Rotkäppchen* – Little Red Riding Hood – a sparkling wine from East Germany) includes a pun on the name of a German brandy, Asbach Uralt, literally 'Ancient Asbach'. Instead of the brand name, however, Sebald playfully writes 'der uralte Asbach', 'the age-old Asbach'.

In the Summer of 1836
VVJ, K&C, H.

The composer Frédéric Chopin (1810–49) fell in love with the sixteen-year-old Maria Wodzińska and, in July 1836, proposed

marriage to her at the White Swan Inn at Marienbad, where the
Wodzińska family was staying. She accepted the engagement,
but her mother, realizing her husband was against the union,
made secrecy the condition of her own consent. The family
returned to Poland in 1837; the plans never came to fruition
and indeed only came to light after Chopin's death with the
discovery among the composer's papers of Maria's letters, in an
envelope which he had marked 'Moja bieda' (my
wretchedness).

In Alfermée
VVJ, K&C, H.

Title: Alfermée is a small village in the Canton of Berne on the
banks of Lake Biel (Bielersee, Lac de Bienne) in Switzerland.

a language you do not understand: Alfermée is the home of the critic
Heinz Schafroth, an expert on the work of the German poet
Günter Eich, whose ashes were scattered by his wife, the writer
Ilse Aichinger, in the vineyards of Alfermée. Sebald visited
Schafroth's house twice: once during the winter of 1997, when
Sebald was holding the lectures at the University of Zürich on
which he would base his book *Luftkrieg und Literatur* (*On the
Natural History of Destruction*); and once in the summer of the
same year, when, accompanied by Heinz Schafroth, he visited
St Peter's Island on Lake Biel, an expedition described in the
second chapter of Sebald's book of essays *Logis in einem Landhaus*
('A Place in the Country'), 1998. According to Schafroth, their
conversation would certainly have included references to the
Austrian writer Marianne Fritz (1948–2007), author of the
three-volume, 3,400-page novel *Dessen Sprache du nicht verstehst*
('Whose Language You Do Not Understand'), published in
1985. Fritz's prose-work *Naturgemäß I* ('By Nature') had
appeared in five volumes in 1996, a year before Sebald's second

visit to Alfermée. The two parts of the *Naturgemäß* project
(*Naturgemäß II* appearing in 1998) went on to make up some
7,000 pages. Heinz Schafroth has confirmed that it is 'not going
too far' to see Marianne Fritz behind the figure of the
exhausted writer (described in German as 'Schreiberin': a
woman writer) in the third stanza of the poem (Heinz
Schafroth: personal communication via Samuel Moser,
1 March 2011).

On the Eve of
VVJ, K&C, H.

In the Paradise Landscape
GG1.
the younger Brueghel: Jan Breughel the Younger was born in
   Antwerp in 1601 and died there in 1678. The painting, in the
   Städel Museum in Frankfurt am Main, is generally referred to
   as *Paradise with the Creation of Eve*. It was probably painted
   towards the end of the 1630s.

Appendix

I remember
P.
Golden Holborn: presumably a conflation of Golden Virginia and
   Old Holborn, two brands of tobacco used to make hand-rolled
   cigarettes.